D1388518

VOICES OF FEMINIST THERAPY

VOICES OF FEMINIST THERAPY

Edited by

Elizabeth Friar Williams

harwood academic publishers

Australia China France Germany India Japan Luxembourg
Malaysia The Netherlands Russia Singapore Switzerland
Thailand United Kingdom United States

3 Boulevard Royal
L-2449 Luxembourg

British Library Cataloguing in Publication Data

Voices of Feminist Therapy
I. Williams, Elizabeth Friar
616.8914082

ISBN   3-7186-0603-8   (hardcover)
       3-7186-0604-6   (softcover)

To

Sara E. Friar and Claudia A. Friar

Growing up fast in a world we made better for them

CONTENTS

INTRODUCTION

Feminist therapy is a revolutionary therapeutic modality, which, to its proponents, means not only a technique but also a theory of individual and social change. Most directly, its roots are in radical therapy promulgated by Szasz (1961) and Laing (1967). The consciousness-raising movement of the 1960s and early 1970s[1] also contributed to the underpinnings of feminist therapy, particularly in their appreciation of the therapeutic value of women recognizing the commonality of their negative experiences as women who grew up in a patriarchal society. No longer would a woman's psychological distress be viewed as her unique intrapsychic neurosis—Freud's famous wars among the id, ego, and superego—but as the natural response of healthy organisms to society's and family's restrictive demands for women's behavior. To put it concisely, society wanted to keep women in a relatively powerless position vis-à-vis men: controlled by them and dependent on them for approval and financial support.

Standards of mental health for women emphasized the qualities that men wanted and needed in women. The result was that women who could not or would not meet those standards suffered from the anger and abuse, emotional and physical, of frustrated men, as well as from rejection from male intimates, co-workers, and bosses. Women who were angrier than men wanted them to be; fatter than men wanted them to be; less sexually available than men wanted them to be; more successful in their careers than men wanted them to be; less "attractive," facially, than men wanted them to be, more sexually assertive than men wanted them to be; more argumentative; more "independent,"and so on, were told they were "disturbed," "inadequate," "frigid," "hysterical," "crazy," "lesbian," and "selfish." Of course women became depressed, angry, and physically symptomatic as a result of such labeling from people they loved or once loved. Worse, such women had no place to go for emotional support. The therapists, physicians, and clergyman—almost exclusively male—whom a physically and emotionally hurt woman sought out for advice or comfort generally agreed with society's and her husband's or parents' assessment of her as emotionally disturbed and urged or forced her to undergo "treatment." These "therapies"—shock treatments; lobotomies; isolation in "rest homes" or sanitaria; medication; or at best (for rich women) "simply" long-term, expensive, time-consuming psychoanalysis—focused on her "neuroses" and helped her blame herself and absolve anyone else from responsibility for her distress. Already invalidated as a reliable source of information about herself and others because of her "mental disturbance," the woman in analysis was further invalidated by the signal technique of the psychoanalyst: the "analysis of the transference." This technique implies that patients' feelings towards and reaction to the therapist are based entirely on their *distortions* of the therapist's behavior and personality, since the therapist made himself almost completely an unknown quantity to his patients. At least that was the ideal. We now know how many male therapists (still) make themselves all *too* well known to their emotionally dependent female patients!

Until the late 1960s and early 1970s, most therapists saw the goals of a woman's therapy as the ability to be married happily, to have "vaginal" orgasms, and to be fulfilled by motherhood, presumably a "natural" state for them. The wife and mother roles were viewed by male "experts" as the ultimate expression of woman's aspirations and those who turned away from these identities were diagnosed as suffering from "masculine protest" (neurotic rebellion against their "normal" female destiny). The numbers of women who came to therapy because they "couldn't get married" were legion. Today it is almost laughable—except for the number of ruined lives that must be represented—to read case histories before the mid-1970s that invariably ended with the therapist writing: "She resolved her neurotic conflicts and was able to marry happily. When I last heard from her she had just had her 2nd child." (Of course, therapists never reported their "failures," i.e.: women who resisted society's domestic goals for them.)

"There must be something wrong with me" was the first statement of most women in therapy, trained to look at their own deficiencies as the causes of their unhappiness and, indeed, trained to be depressed if others in their intimate lives were not happy with them![2] I remember a female client, a lawyer, who brought her lover to one of her sessions. As soon as they sat down, she turned to the man and said, in all seriousness, "Tell Betsy what's wrong with me." If I hadn't interrupted this exchange, he would have.

Feminist therapy, alone, promised a way out of this dilemma. Feminist therapy taught women that what would help them was the feminist analysis of society that showed them how society caused their suffering, how their socialization as "good girls" had made them "sick," and how their symptoms were actually signs of health—symbolic of their rebellion against these strictures. How the early feminist therapists characterized this task emerges from this collection of essays.

The first piece, by Sarah Pearlman, personifies the early idealism and radical goals of the feminist therapists and how these evolved over time. As feminist therapists age, their personal needs and commitment of energy, of course, changes, and this is illustrated especially by Polly Taylor's and Adrienne Smith's essays.

Early experiences in the crucible of the family that motivated radicalism, rebellion, and a specifically feminist reaction in the feminist therapist's ideological and psychological development are illustrated in particular by my "story" and that of Joan Hamerman Robbins.

The transition from radical activist politics to feminist therapy with a specific group of disenfranchised citizens is demonstrated by Joan Saks Berman; Maria Fadli also describes working with a poor, under-served population in a treatment facility that had been, until her arrival, entirely indifferent to and ignorant about the needs of female clients. Jeanne Adleman, still working as a feminist counselor at age seventy-five, also began her young adult life in radical politics. She then moved through a career in education, always in the service of humanistic goals, often challenging "received wisdom," and asking whether a particular practice or ideology would be good for women and children before many others thought about these things.

Important to the history of feminist therapy are the organizations that supported and involved the early feminist therapists—all, of course, created by them, sometimes together with female psychologists from disciplines other than therapy—the Association for Women in Psychology (AWP) was founded at the outset for therapists who were not necessarily psychologists and for feminist social scientists and educators. Several of the contributors to this book were active in founding and later in sustaining some of these organizations, for example: Barbara Sang, who describes her experiences in the early days of AWP and the NOW Psychotherapy Referral Service. I, too, was an early member of both those groups, my experience of the latter being different from Barbara's. Doris Howard has been active on the steering committees of both the Feminist Therapy Institute and AWP and is the recipient of the latter's highest award for her outstanding contribution to the Association: the Christine Ladd-Franklin award.

Some feminist therapists in the early years disdained academic degrees and licensing because they wanted to stress their similarities to and identification with their clients. They did not want to be viewed by them, as were therapists from the "establishment," as "authorities" or "professionals." While all the therapists represented in this book were superbly trained as clinicians and as feminist therapists (mostly training themselves in the latter practice), not all chose to be licensed. To some, that implied a conformity to authoritarian standards they felt irrelevant to helping women achieve better mental health. Indeed, as we have seen, licensing as a mental health clinician has not prevented horrific abuses, both sexual and emotional, of female clients.

The geographic, class, and family backgrounds of the feminist therapists represented in this book are diverse, a wonderful challenge to stereotypes of feminists. While Ida Truscott was the daughter of a farm family, Barbara Sang was raised in New York City. Maria Fadli came from Puerto Rico and Ann McClenahan was a child of a conservative Republican family from a prairie state where she still lives and often must answer the question: "What's a feminist therapist doing in South Dakota?" Jeanne Adleman's father died when she was six, an event that forced her mother and two aunts and their families to live together, and even then, food on the table was problematic. Doris Howard lost her father at thirteen, and also lost the attentions of her childlike mother, too consumed with her own loss to care for the needs of her two grieving daughters. I came from an intact family that was economically privileged, but emotionally impoverished.

Diversity is also represented in the intimate relationships that are described or can be inferred from these memoirs. Some feminist therapists in these pages are lesbian; some are married; some were previously married but now have found alternate arrangements that suit them better; several live alone and seem satisfied not to be in an intimate relationship; some are living alone but obviously are connected intimately to someone who remains anonymous in these pages. Several of the therapists are mothers with grown or growing children and a couple, including myself, are grandmothers.

What these women seem to have in common, first of all, is their extraordinary resilience, a concept only recently coming into prominence in psychological literature. None had ideal families; none had all or even most of their psychological needs met, far from it. Several were abused emotionally, if not physically. Yet instead of becoming embittered, depressed, or emotionally disorganized, they became fighters, creators, and lovers. The other quality that seems to be shared by many of the feminist therapists in these pages is the willingness to take risks. I think of Kayla Weiner, whose mother was crippled when Kayla was five years old, whose parents urged her into teaching, the "safe" career desired for us by many of our parents in the days when "real women" were supposed to look for protection and a risk-free lifestyle. At first acquiescing and becoming a teacher, Kayla soon rebelled totally, running away, as she puts it, to cross the country with her two cats and a newly purchased van. I went to New York at age twenty-four with my little son, age five, without a job, without a place to live, and stayed there thirty-one years, growing up in the process.

All of the therapists in this book were brave in their choices of mates or lifestyles or education and not least, in choosing to practice a new, unsung type of psychotherapy, which offered them not material rewards, such as traditional therapists sought, but the reward of participating actively in a great political and social movement that promised to improve all women's emotional health.

A NOTE ON THE SELECTION OF CONTRIBUTORS

I put flyers in the AWP–APA hospitality suite at the annual conventions for two years asking for contributors to a book about the history of feminist therapy, who would be willing to speak personally about their development as feminist therapists and their places in the history of feminist therapy. A similar request was made in several issues of the newsletters of the Feminist Therapy Institute, the Association for Women in Psychology, and the Division of the Psychology of Women (Div. 35) of the American Psychological Association. From approximately 150 replies I chose 25, and from the 25 chose those appearing in this book for their interesting information about the early days of feminist therapy, their skill in writing, their openness, their diversity, and their ability to inspire those who we hope will follow.

NOTES

1. Anita Shreve, in her important book, *Women Together, Women Alone, the Legacy of the Consciousness-Raising Movement* (New York: Viking, 1989), places the CR movement's beginning in 1967, its "heyday" in 1972 and 1973 (14) and its demise in 1980.
2. Ellen Kaschak's article, *"Feminist Psychotherapy; The First Decade"* in *Female Psychology, The Emerging Self,* E. Cox (ed.) (New York: St. Martin's, 1981), is an excellent summary of the early years of feminist therapy.

REFERENCES

Laing, R.D. *The Divided Self.* London: Tavistock,1967.
Szasz. T.T. *The Myth of Mental Illness.* New York: Harper and Row,. 1961.

ACKNOWLEDGMENTS

I'd like to express my appreciation to the members of the feminist therapy community in Northern California who have extended a warm welcome to me in my new home. In particular, Doris Howard, Jeanne Adleman, and Joan Robbins. Barbara Sang, an old friend from New York days, has remained a strong supporter since we were both in the early NOW psychotherapy community. Several colleagues on the AWP Implementation Collective (IMPS) made work fun and gave me a lot to think about as we met in locales as disparate as Northern Mexico and Indianapolis. Joan Chrisler, Ruth Hall, Carla Golden, Pat Rozee, Maureen McHugh, Donna Hawxhurst, and Susanna Rose come to mind, especially. Other AWP members who stimulated my thinking about modern feminism and psychology include: Ellen Kaschak, Joan Saks Berman, Kayla Weiner, and Sue Morrow. I'm proud to be a member (one of the first members) of this remarkable organization as we celebrate our 25th year!

With their consistent support and friendliness, my colleagues in the Northern California chapter of the American Society of Journalists and Authors made it possible for me to change painlessly my professional focus from therapist to author/editor and writing teacher. I think especially of Shari Steiner, Shannon Moffat, Shimon-Craig Van Collie, Norma Peterson, Maxine Cass, and Fred Gebhart.

Florence Williams, the finest writer I know, has acted as an "unofficial" editor, providing affection and advice. I thank her, as well.

CONTRIBUTORS

Jeanne Adleman has a consulting practice in San Francisco specializing in feminist therapy issues. She is also an educator, writer, and editor. Her most recent work, co-edited with G. Enguidanos, is *Racism in the Lives of Women: Testimony, Theory, and Guide to Anti-Racist Practice* (Harrington Park Press/Haworth, 1995).

Joan Saks Berman works with the Indian Health Service. She is active in the Feminist Therapy Institute, has written on ethical issues in psychotherapy, and is editing a forthcoming book on therapy issues relevant to women of color.

Maria Fadli practiced feminist therapy in a drug treatment center in New York City for many years. Now living in San Francisco, she assists those who have been persecuted in other countries to make application for immigration to the United States. She is a member of the Association for Women in Psychology.

Doris K. Howard was in practice in New York City from 1970 to 1988. At present she is living and practicing in San Francisco, where she is clinical supervisor at a residential facility for people in crisis. She has served on the steering committee of the Feminist Therapy Institute and on the Implementation Collective of the Association for Women in Psychology. She has been an editor of the journal *Women and Therapy.*

Lee Johnson-Kaufmann has been a public health nurse and is now in private practice in Danville, California. She is currently writing a play-book on sex therapy for therapists and couples.

Ann McClenahan practices feminist therapy in South Dakota. She is a member of the Association for Women in Psychology.

Sarah F. Pearlman is an assistant professor in the Doctoral program in Clinical Psychology at the University of Hartford and maintains a private practice in Hartford. She is an editor and author of articles in *The Anthology of Lesbian Psychologies*. (University of Illinois Press, 1987).

Joan Hamerman Robbins is in private practice in San Francisco and lives in Bodega Bay, California. She is an author, most recently of *Knowing Herself: Women Tell Their Stories in Psychotherapy* (Insight Books, 1991), and a member of the Feminist Therapy Institute.

Barbara E. Sang is currently in practice in New York City. She has written many articles on art and psychotherapy and on lesbian issues in psychology and psychotherapy. With Adrienne Smith and Joyce Warshow, she has published *Lesbians at Midlife: The Creative Transition* (Spinsters' Book Co., 1991). She is a member of the Association for Women in Psychology.

Adrienne J. Smith, who died in 1991, was one of the founders of the Feminist Therapy Institute. She said she was a lesbian before she was a therapist and a feminist after both. She combined all three identities to become the first openly lesbian therapist in Chicago. She was actively involved in Division 44 of APA, serving as its president from 1988 to 1990. She co-edited, with Barbara E. Sang and Joyce Warshow, *Lesbians at Midlife: The Creative Transition* (Spinsters' Book Co., *1991*).

Polly E. Taylor lives in San Francisco, where she publishes the nationally known feminist journal, *Broomstick*. Formerly, she practiced feminist therapy and is now administrator of the Feminist Therapy Institute.

Ida P. Truscott was born in farm country early in the century. She now lives and practices half the year in Snowmass Village, Colorado, and half in Cardiff-by-the-Sea, California. She is a member of the Association for Women in Psychology.

Kayla Weiner has a private practice in Seattle. She writes and lectures about the psychology of Jewish women and about anti-Semitism in the field of psychology. Her four favorite things are sitting in front of the fire with her cat on her lap, reading a good book, being with friends, and traveling to exotic places around the world. She is the editor of *Jewish Women Speak Out: Expanding the Boundaries of Psychology* (Canopy Press, Seattle, 1995).

Elizabeth Friar Williams was in practice from 1969–1986 in New York City where she wrote *Notes of a Feminist Therapist*, (Praeger, 1976; Dell, 1977), the first book about social-psychological issues in psychotherapy of women clients. She now lives in San Francisco, where she works as an author, co-author, editor, and publisher of books and articles on psychotherapy and education, and teaches writing at the University of San Francisco. From 1991–1994 she was spokesperson for the Association for Women in Psychology and also is a member of the Feminist Therapy Institute.

1

RADICAL ROOTS

1

The Radical Edge: Feminist Therapy as Political Activism

SARAH F. PEARLMAN

There are these moments when you know that how you see the world will never be the same. For me, it was reading "Sisterhood is Powerful"[1] and Adrienne Rich . . . and listening to Meg Christian sing in the small basement of an inner city church.

This article is about my history and changes as a feminist and as a feminist therapist. It is also about my perception and my experience of the radicalization of a community of women who lived in Hartford, Connecticut, during the early and mid-1970s. Thus, my story is part of the history of feminist therapy as well as the history of the beginning of the Second Wave of American feminism.

THE CONTEXT/THE TIMES

I have thought of myself as a feminist since 1971. Like many other women of that particular era, I was a woman who had married too young and had children too early. Although my life in many ways had followed a stereotypical path as wife and mother, my personality has always tended towards the adventurous and iconoclastic so that I had

managed some departures. I had returned to college to finish my degree (unheard of for married women in 1960) . . . and I was not a new-
comer to politics or protest since I had been intensely involved in
anti-Vietnam war organizing and activism.

I was in graduate school in the early 1970s and sitting in classrooms listening to my male professors lecture how mothers were responsible for a vast array of psychological ills including schizo-
phrenia and homosexuality, that responses on psychological ques-
tionnaires that indicated discontent with the female role were signs
of pathology, and that vaginal orgasm was the only normal or mature orgasm. One of my more ironic memories is of proposing to
write a paper on feminist therapy for a course in individual psychotherapy and being turned down. The reason my instructor gave was
that there were too few references and that it was not a viable topic!

America in the early seventies was still reeling from events of the
sixties: the murders of Robert Kennedy and Martin Luther King, the
killing and imprisonment of numerous Black political leaders, ghetto riots across the country, and huge anti-war protest demonstrations. We were still in Vietnam, hopes of a Black power political
movement were fading, and the new left and anti-war protest movement had begun to dissipate. However, it was still the counter-cul-
ture era of hippies, drug use viewed through a lens of fun and
enhancement of experience, and urban and back-to-the-land communes. To remain a traditional wife seemed like terminal imprisonment, and I catapulted (along with many of my friends) out of my
marriage and suburban living into the intoxicating atmosphere of
the second wave of the Women's Liberation Movement.

The concept of sisterhood was then a passionate and powerful
ideal. Health collectives and consciousness-raising groups were
multiplying across the country and there was a critical outpouring of
feminist analysis that attacked every established patriarchal ideology or belief from history to religion to medicine. Our women's bodies were a special site of protest and insistence . . . not only that we
must have the right to reproductive choice, but that knowledge (taking back our bodies from doctor-dominated medicine), pride in our
bodies, and controlling our sexuality was crucial to our freedom. I
was very influenced by the ideas of Wilhelm Reich and was convinced that body shame and repression of sexual desire and the
senses were connected to political domination. Body and sexual liberation, including liberating masturbation, became a revolutionary

obligation and I had few friends who did not possess a collection of menstrual sponges, speculums, and/or vibrators.

Also, Kate Millett[2] had positioned Freud and penis envy squarely in an historical context of over-reaction to both biology and nineteenth century European Feminism (and under-reaction or blindness to male-dominated culture) . . . confirming that psychological theories functioned to maintain male domination and female inferiority. The abuse of women patients/clients (mind-numbing medications, electric shock therapy, sexual abuse by therapists) by the male psychiatric establishment was beginning to be documented.[3] In addition, articles by women psychotherapists[4,5] were confronting traditional sex roles, proposing that the female role be expanded to include such behaviors as assertiveness and mastery. Change, not just adjustment by women to their respective situations, was now the goal of therapy.

By 1974, I was working as a consultant to a rape crisis service. It was devastating to listen to the stories of the women who had been viciously assaulted, to hear their terror and shame, and to see how they were mistreated in hospital emergency rooms, by police, and later in the courtroom . . . and to know that their rapist was walking around free. Women who were beaten by husbands and boyfriends were beginning to call the service and some women were disclosing incest. I don't remember exactly when I and my co-workers began to comprehend that rape was not random, but epidemic and that what we were observing was an institutionalized acceptance of violence towards women, and a legal system that served to protect male privilege, including sexual privilege. This changed us all . . . a change leading to a feminism that was becoming increasingly anti-male.

Concurrent with anti-rape organizing, the Hartford Women's Center became a primary meeting place and center of feminist activities for women. Jill Johnston was one invited speaker, leaving in her wake such concepts as lesbian nation and that revolutionary feminism and heterosexuality were contradictions. Lesbianism became a strong political stand and fewer heterosexual women were attending Center events as lesbians began to take the organizing lead. In addition, along with the emergence of separatism and other radical lesbian feminist beliefs, there became an intensification of an ideology of political purity or correctness. And together with many of my previously married heterosexual friends, I began to at first identify politically with lesbianism, then fell in love with a woman, and came out.

In essence, I was part of a community of women who had become politically radicalized. A more revolutionary feminism had replaced our initial liberal feminist beliefs and ideals. Many of us had come out as lesbians and the issue was no longer equality. A sense of deep comraderie and joyousness matched our political seriousness and we believed that we were taking back our lives. We wanted a new world. What we wanted was the end of the patriarchy (and the end of capitalism).

FEMINIST THERAPY: THE RADICAL EDGE

By the mid seventies, mimeographed articles on a more radical brand of feminist therapy were being distributed by feminist therapy collectives and study groups around the country as the Women's Liberation Movement moved from a liberal to a more radical understanding and position on women's oppression. Although there was an ongoing debate about whether male-oriented psychological theories could be revised and made useful for women, a new feminist therapy was emerging. This new therapy was anti-theoretical, anti-male, and anti-power in reaction to both a traditional psychology which inferiorized women and separated the understanding of people from the real conditions of their lives . . . and a traditional psychotherapy, which repeated the power relations between women and men in an exploitive therapy milieu.

Traditional psychotherapy was viewed as conducted by a (mostly) male authority figure who remained personally anonymous, listened to his clients through a harmful-to-women (classical psychoanalytic) theory, considered himself an expert on the female experience, and was part of a professional elite which mystified and concealed knowledge. He interpreted his (female) client's motivations, told her what her experience was (or should be), labeled all reactions or unwanted/undesirable behaviors towards him as transference, and pathologized the client through disconnecting her struggles (called "symptoms") from the political realities of poverty, race, class, role, gender oppression, heterosexism, and powerlessness.

The goal of this new feminist therapy was no longer individualistic or "personalist"; that is, self-actualization through expansion of the feminine role. Our vision now was to help women change their lives and to politicize them in the process. Thus, I learned and practiced a feminist therapy based on such concepts as: all personal experience was political, that women were healthy, and that it was the complex destructiveness of female socialization and the role which were sick. The major concept which informed feminist therapy was that of the empowerment of women. I believed that this was achieved primarily through egalitarianism or "de-powering" the therapy relationship, and by returning authority to woman through viewing the client as an expert on herself. Empowerment meant normalizing women's experience and reactions in order to decrease self-blame, encouraging connection with other women and a women-identified identity (that is, identifying with all women as a class), facilitating political understanding of personal experience, and encouraging participation in community activities and ultimately engagement in feminist activism. I believed that lesbianism was a more normal sexual/relational life choice than heterosexuality (there was a time when I believed that all of my clients should withdraw from men and come out as lesbians). I thought that women should end abusive relationships and I encouraged relational empowerment through behaviors that included assertiveness, limit setting, and the direct expression of feelings including anger.

To equalize or balance the therapist/client relationship, I would frequently self-disclose to establish commonality and make myself known as a person who had experienced similar difficulties and struggles, believing that this reduced self-condemnation in clients and increased their hopes for change. In addition, I looked for opportunities to demystify (teach) therapy and would explain my thinking or observations that led me to insights and interventions. However, I believed that my primary task as a feminist therapist was to facilitate **political** understanding of the woman's problems. Thus, I would point out the commonalities of problems and experiences that I thought most women shared. In addition, I would affirm reactions to struggles and conditions as understandable and appropriate in order to de-pathologize the woman and reduce her tendency towards self-blame.

Also, I would often utilize alternative therapies such as Gestalt and bio-energetics and believed in a mind-body approach; specifically that the body was the physical manifestation of personality through muscular structuring. I was convinced that female subordination was structured in women's bodies and lodged in feminine mannerisms, that women's bodies needed to change in order for women to change, and would frequently recommend self-defense training in order for the woman to achieve a new and more powerful sense of her body. Also, many women were then pre-orgasmic due to sexual misinformation (orgasm through heterosexual intercourse), and teaching women how to have orgasm and to sexualize one's body through sensualizing techniques and masturbation was often an important part of therapy.

Another primary feminist belief was that therapy should be accessible to everyone so that important issues were money and fees. This meant that I needed to balance my need to make a living with what clients could afford and I attempted to do this through a policy of negotiating or adjusting fees downward during times of financial strain (as well as occasional bartering). In addition, my vision of feminist therapy included being a resource on events and activities and I would encourage joining consciousness-raising groups, participating in community activities, and establishing friendships with other women in order to build relational resources and women identification. Since I was an active participant in my community, my clients and I were often part of the same social network. Personal/professional boundaries did not seem that important and some of my clients became friends after therapy ended. Actually, professionalism was quite suspect during those times and formal professional training was not considered necessary to gain skill as a therapist (opinions which were personally offensive to me since I had worked hard to complete graduate training).

Overall, the vision of the radical edge of feminist therapy (a blending of feminism and radical therapy) was to free women from destructive socializing influences, help them to change their personal lives, encourage them to learn to work collectively and cooperatively with other women, increase their political awareness, and facilitate their eventual participation in political activism. To me and other radical feminists, feminist therapy as means to individual personal change was not enough. Feminist therapists were to be agents of political change and politicalization, and political activism was thought of as the crucial end point in healing or recovering from female socialization. My sustained belief was that therapy could serve to help women in their journey towards political consciousness and that women clients would become part of a revolutionary movement and add to our growing numbers who were struggling to end patriarchy.

NEW CONTEXTS/NEW UNDERSTANDINGS: MAINTAINING FEMINIST INTEGRITY

By the late seventies, the ideal of sisterhood and the sense of oneness or the sameness of all women faded as assertions of race, class, and ethnic difference began to emerge. These assertions unveiled a feminism which had been based on white, middle class values and privileges, and was frequently irrelevant to African-American and other minority women. While a feminist (psychoanalytic) psychology of women had evolved,[6,7] its theory and practice reflected the overall limitations of feminist thinking, overgeneralizing experience, not accounting for differences between women, and pseudo-including women from other backgrounds and cultures. What had become apparent was that gender was not always the primary site of identity, loyalty, or oppression for women . . . particularly when more immediate and traumatic oppressions were prevalent. In addition, the feminist movement had splintered into multiple factions and fragmentation increased as communities and groups polarized around a variety of ideological issues (separatism, pornography, transsexuals).

Although feminist ideas of equality in both public and private relational life had entered national and global consciousness and some legislative changes had occurred, the entrenchment and resiliency of the patriarchal/capitalist power structures remained the same. In addition, while some women were able to attain success and affluence, recessions began to cycle into the economy. The feminization of poverty became an increasing reality and female economic dependency accelerated as the economy and then opportunity declined.

I had also begun to understand that women came into therapy, not to be politicized by a therapist or to change the world, but to have their personal world change and to feel differently about themselves. Personal consciousness re-took the lead over political consciousness and the radical edge subsided as feminist therapy returned to its initial "individualistic" position. And as I changed with the times and with age and experience, new realizations emerged. I was beginning to see that a strictly feminist approach was insufficient . . . particularly for women who had grown up in chaotic and abusive surroundings and who were left with vulnerabilities and struggles which made functioning and emotional survival extremely difficult. Also, it was becoming clear to me that I needed additional ways to understand and to respond in therapy, and I gradually evolved a framework which merged feminist thinking with a revised psychodynamic approach (primarily object relations and self-psychology theories).

In addition, as I watched the economic situation change, I saw that leaving problematic relationships, even abusive ones, was a highly personal and frightening decision . . . and that women who ended marriages without financial and relational resources entered a situation of extreme hardship, emotional as well as economic. Another realization was that what was erotic was different for different women, that heterosexuality was not simply sexual repression, and that not all women would become lesbians. I learned also that power is clearly inherent in the therapist/client relationship, but that it does not have to be abusive or exploitive. Rather, it can be the kind of power or influence that helps people to change in the ways they want. And I began to understand my own need for personal and professional boundaries and that therapy could be adversely affected by confounding roles.

Yet, those radical years were the years when I was most myself and my work most congruent with what I believed. I am a very different therapist now. However, it has not been easy to redefine therapy, relinquish polarized beliefs, maintain a sense of integrity or sustain some political vision in these hard times of counter-reaction, reduced opportunity, social manipulation and governmental unresponsiveness. Nor is it easy to lose a dream and struggle with feelings of betrayal, yet remain intensely visionary in how I believe women's lives should be.

REFERENCES

1. Morgan, Robin (Ed). 1970. *Sisterhood is powerful: An anthology of writings from the Women's Liberation Movement.* NY: Basic Books.
2. Millett, Kate. (1970). *Sexual politics.* NY: Doubleday & Co. Inc.
3. Chesler, Phyllis. (1972). *Women and madness.* Garden City: Doubleday.
4. Kronsky, Betty. (1971). Feminism and Psychotherapy. *Journal of Contemporary Psychotherapy, 3,* 2, 89–98.
5. Shainess, Natalie. (1970). Is there a separate feminine psychology? *New York State Journal of Medicine, 70,* 24, 3007–3009.
6. Chodorow, Nancy. (1978). *The reproduction of mothering: Psychoanalysis and the sociology of gender.* Berkeley: Univ. of California Press.
7. Euchenbaum, Luise & Orbach, Susie. (1983). *Understanding women: A feminist psychoanalytic approach.* NY: Basic Books.

2

From Chicago to Rainbow Bridge: In Search of Changing Woman

JOAN SAKS BERMAN

Changing Woman is one of the Holy People in Navajo mythology, perhaps the principal figure among them. Kin'aalda, the female puberty ceremony was first performed for her. She was involved in the creation of the Earth Surface People, creating the first four clans from parts of her body. She was also involved with the meeting at which they were taught how to control the wind, lightining, storms, and animals.

Rainbow Bridge is a rock formation considered by some to be one of the Navajo holy places. Since the construction of the Glen Canyon Dam and creation of Lake Powell, it is reachable only by boat, or by hiking with backpack for 2½ days.

This was the beginning paragraph of a paper I wrote about my work with Native American women, which was first presented at the Advanced Feminist Therapy Institute (AFTI) and the Association for Women in Psychology (AWP) annual conference. The paper was later presented at conferences in Managua, Nicaragua in 1987 and in Sidney, Australia in 1988, and after many revisions, was published in *Women and therapy* in 1989. The published version has the title, "View from Rainbow Bridge: feminist therapist meets Changing Woman." I began working for the Indian Health Service on the Navajo and Hopi reservations in June, 1980. When I first left Chicago, my birthplace, for the Arizona desert, I felt as if I were going off on a Peace Corps assignment because I was going to an area that was geographically alien, to work with people whose native languages were not English, and whose culture and religion were unfamiliar. I wondered if I would be able to bridge the cultural gap in order to empathize with the emotional concerns of the people who would come to me for help. I saw this as crucial, since my previous experience with ethnic and racial minorities in an urban environment had led me to understand how culture can influence the way an individual defines her identity and self-concept. I also recognize some of the effects of being a member of a group that is discriminated against by the larger society. I see myself as a minority because of my Jewish heritage as well as because of my feminist beliefs, so I found it strange, once I was on the reservation, to be perceived as an Anglo, a representative of the dominant though somewhat external culture. My feminist perspective has aided me in seeing the similarities as well as the differences in working with women of another ethnic group.

Tuba City Indian Hospital had never had a feminist therapist on the staff, and word got around fast, for better or worse, without my having to advertise my orientation. It is my belief that a feminist integrates her politics into all aspects of her life, so that it's demonstrated by her behavior, and others soon come to recognize this.

I began working with battered women who were referred from the medical clinic, and unsuccessfully tried to get a group started, for there were more than enough referrals of this kind. Angie, a college student in the CETA summer intern program sought me out to be her supervisor while she did the groundwork for a battered women's shelter. (The one in Flagstaff had not yet opened). Angie, a Navajo whose family lived there, went back to school in Flagstaff, but her work was continued by a couple of VISTA volunteers. We formed the Committee Against Spouse Abuse, and later participated in a Northern Arizona Task Force, a coalition of similar groups in communities both on and off reservations. I also was invited to speak on the psychological aspects of rape victims and their families during an all-day in-service training seminar on rape and sexual assault for hospital and school personnel.

I began studying the Navajo language at the local branch of the community college. The classes actually met in the High School in the evening. Navajo is a difficult language to learn and because of this was used to relay secret radio messages during World War II. I read that it requires right hemisphere functioning of the brain, in contrast to most language ability, which takes place in the left hemisphere. I hoped that as a left-handed, right-brained person I would have an advantage! It was my idea that some familiarity with the language would demonstrate a cultural awareness that would help me understand clients (although Navajo interpreters were available when necessary). Among other things, Navajo, like Chinese and other Asian languages, does not differentiate gender in third person pronouns, so in English, *he* and *she* might be used inter-changeably.

One of the activities of my job was to make home visits, often useful in facilitating follow-up on clients. It was a way to experience first-hand the isolation of a remote rural hogan (traditional style home) and the rustic living conditions, so different from the comfort and convenience of offices and middle class, urban style housing. I feel I was lucky to live in government housing, with electricity and telephones, and didn't have to haul water from miles away or chop wood for heat and cooking. The clients who came to the clinic had to travel long distances on dirt roads. There was no public transportation and frequently clients had no money for gas or, indeed, no regular transportation except walking or hitchhiking.

After I tried taking the oral exam for licensure in the State of California I knew that the kind of work I was doing and the conditions of the environment were not well understood by the establishment professional community. I had already spent several years in Tuba City and wanted to move on because my patriarchal, autocratic psychiatrist boss was bad for my mental health. As part of the oral exam, I had to present a case from my practice. I described a battered woman who, with my help, had been able to establish a life away from her abusive husband. The critique I received of my presentation included such remarks as: "Performing like a social worker" because I instructed her in how to get food stamps and look for a job so she could support her children. I was also told that I didn't "demonstrate sufficient cultural sensitivity" although I was living immersed in the culture! Of course, during the exam I didn't think it was appropriate to talk about my leisure time activities, which included attending kachina dances in the Hopi villages, and all night Yei Bi Chai dances, a healing ceremony performed at the annual Western Navajo Fair. Perhaps I should have worn my turquoise necklace, tiered skirt, and handmade moccasins (an outfit which caused one of my feminist colleagues to ask if I had "gone native") to the exam. When I finally left, it was by transferring to another Indian Health Service location in Albuquerque, where I am now. But in another sense, it was a longer road which took me to this place.

Once, when I was in an encounter group workshop, I participated in a life-planning exercise that required me to write my own eulogy. Writing a memoir is something like that exercise, constructing by oneself, not only one's memories, but the ways one would like to be remembered.

Going back in the time machine, I remember when I first realized I was a feminist, which was Labor Day weekend, 1967. Prior to that time I had been a political activist, probably starting with the Congress on Racial Equality (CORE) sit-ins at the University of Chicago in 1961, protesting the University's segregated housing policies. In May, 1965, I was arrested in Chicago's first anti-Vietnam War demonstration, after we sat down in the middle of State and Madison at 4:00 on a Friday afternoon. The arrests were immortalized in Studs Terkel's book, *Division street: America* (pp.85–101) in his interview with Eva Barnes, who joined our demonstration. Shortly after the arrest for disorderly conduct, my FBI file was started. In the fall, when I started to work on my doctorate at Northwestern University, I applied for a position as psychological assistant at the VA in order to support myself as I was going through school. At the time, the federal government employment form (SF-171) asked if you had ever been *arrested* (not convicted) for anything besides a traffic violation. The case had not yet gone to trial, so I thought I had best be honest. I described the reason for the arrest. Although in court we were convicted of blocking traffic and charged a $25 fine (the amount of our bail), the ball had already started rolling. The FBI interviewed my parents' neighbors and all my past employers, back to the time I was in high school, but no one would say that I was a subversive.

During the next few years, I was active in Citizens for Independent Political Action (CIPA), a neighborhood organizing group. One of the other women in the group had read Betty Friedan's *The Feminine mystique* and had joined NOW, but when she talked about the issues, I didn't think they pertained to me. After all, I was a graduate student preparing for a professional career, not a housewife with children. It was as a representative of CIPA that I attended the National Conference for New Politics in September, 1967. Madalyn Murray O'Hare called a women's caucus and it was during that meeting that I had my "click" experience. It suddenly became clear to me that if I was a full time graduate student and worked 20 hours a week in the VA Mental Health Clinic, I shouldn't also be expected to do all the housework, cooking and laundry while my husband watched television or went to visit his buddies. The next time that he complained that he didn't have clean socks, I told him he could do the laundry himself.

Not long after, the women of CIPA formed a consciousness-raising group (called rap groups in Chicago). In November, 1969, after a weekend conference at a rural retreat center, the Chicago Women's Liberation Union (CWLU) was formed out of the various rap groups around the city. The CWLU was from the beginning an anti-racist, anti-imperialist, and anti-capitalist organization and addressed itself actively to consciousness-raising and other feminist agenda items, such as: equal pay for equal work, the legalization of abortion, and organizing neighborhood and workplace groups of women. The word "feminism" as we use it now was not in common usage at the time, especially among young revolutionaries. From the left (male-dominated) point of view, feminism was a "bourgeois liberal" movement, a phrase frequently applied pejoratively by radicals on the Left.

A few months earlier, in 1969, a group of women and men, psychologists, social workers, and "para-professional" mental health workers, who worked at the state mental hospital and community mental health centers, organized a radical therapy collective, questioning the authoritarian and patriarchal stance of established treatment approaches and attempting to develop new ones embodying more democratic principles. The community psychology movement was gaining momentum and the back wards of the ancient state hospital, with their hydrotherapy and electroshock therapy rooms, were being closed down, now that people could be restrained by chemicals and didn't need locked doors to protect society from them.

It was during this time of social protest and the anti-war movement that Psychologists for Social Action (PSA) got started, and within that organization, a Women's Consortium was formed in March, 1969. We decided to plan a symposium for the American Psychological Association annual meeting in August, 1969, in Washington, D.C. The title was "Woman as Subject," as opposed to women as sex objects. Since the symposium was not sponsored by one of the existing divisions of the organization, it was not listed in the official program. Instead, we plastered the public areas of the hotels with flyers advertising the event. and 400 people, mostly women, showed up. As amazing as this was to us, there were also two other workshops and paper sessions organized by women in other cities. The symposium presented by the Chicago group, which I chaired, discussed (1) the socialization of women and girl children, (2) the Women's Liberation Movement, (3) alternatives to marriage, (4) women in work and employment, (5) demythologizing sex-role stereotypes, and (6) female sexuality.

During the discussion, women started talking about discrimination that they had experienced in school, the job market, and in APA itself. During the sessions, several petitions were circulated for signatures, demanding that APA revise its accreditation procedures to include an examination of discriminatory policies against women in the psychology department being evaluated for accreditation. Other petitions demanded that APA examine its own practices to eliminate discrimination against women in its membership and services it offers, and urging APA to pass a resolution to the effect that abortion (still illegal at that time) be considered a civil right of pregnant women. The women who were in the central core of the excitement continued to meet in someone's hotel room, and it was out of this that the Association for Women in Psychology was born. Elaine Stocker and I wrote a description of these historic events which was published in *Women: A journal of liberation* (Winter, 1970). We had many long, laborious meetings forming and re-forming the structure of the organization and re-writing the by-laws, because birthing a non-hierarchical, feminist organization was not an easy thing, and we had few models. The Chicago women's caucus of PSA became one of the chapters of the organization. Because we already had experience in dealing with conflict and working together collectively, we were seen as a strong power within the AWP organization, sometimes being referred to as the "Chicago Monolith". We wrote papers on feminist psychology and feminist process together for future APA conventions, and we taught a course, "Psychology for Sisters," in the Liberation School of the CWLU. This was before women's studies programs existed in universities; as a group, we were inventing it as we went. As readings we used mimeographed and ditto copies of papers from feminist publications. There weren't many copy machines around yet and few books on the subject had been published.

Shortly after AWP's 1970 mid-winter business meeting, my husband and I went to Cuba with the Venceremos Brigade, to cut sugar cane in international solidarity. Travel to Cuba was forbidden by the U.S. government, but because of a court ruling, it was only illegal to take one's passport there. Transportation was difficult, however.

The Chicago contingent traveled by chartered bus to St. John's, New Brunswick, Canada, to board a Cuban ship. In spite of heavy security training and efforts to keep our departure secret, FBI agents stood at the bottom of the escalator in the Greyhound station, snapping the photos of each of us as we descended to the departure gates. Our cover story was that we were going on a skiing trip to Canada, but it was transparently fiction, since we didn't carry any skis with us. We spent the night locked in a liberal church in Boston, where we were to meet another group. By then our cover had been blown, and as we boarded the buses in the morning, TV reporters stuck microphones in our faces, asking questions about us. When I returned home two months later, my co-workers in the Mental Health Center told me that everyone knew where I went. The ship we traveled on had been converted from a cattle ship in seven days. Five hundred of us, North Americans and Cubans, slept in bunk-beds dormitory style, and bathed in group showers whenever we could brave the cold to get undressed.

The work of cutting sugar cane with a machete was the hardest work I've ever done, and my feet were swollen and blistered most of the six weeks we worked. I was usually so exhausted that I wasn't able to stay up at night to enjoy the entertainment provided us: old Charlie Chaplin classics or Cuban dance bands. This was also an intensely political experience, extending into the two weeks of travel throughout the island after our work was done. In our direct work with the Cubans as well as from the lectures provided for us on Cuban government, health care, education and many other aspects of Cuban life, I learned that a socialist revolution was not enough in itself to completely transform the condition of women in a society, although Cuban's women's lives were markedly improved in material ways. (Details of my observations were published in *Women: A journal of liberation* (Summer, 1970) and later quoted in Sheila Rowbotham's book, *Women, resistance and revolution*. It was now clear to me that my political priority would be working for women in the process of changing society, whether or not we would ever have the kind of revolution which took place in Cuba. As we left Cuba, standing on the deck of our again reconverted cattle ship as we pulled out of the Havana harbor, I had the feeling that I was leaving home to go off to fight the Crusades in the "belly of the monster."

Returning to Chicago and to my job with the Illinois Department of Mental Health, and political activity with the CWLU, I felt like an alien from another planet, something like the experience experi-

enced by one of the characters in Doris Lessing's *The Four-Gated City*.
It seemed that even women's fashionable clothes were a frivolous af-
fectation when a "plain brown wrapper" was all that was necessary.

In June 1971, my husband and I separated after nine years of marriage. We had no children, and since I had been the main breadwinner for much of the time, it was an intensely emotional experience,
but not an economic hardship for me. I started saving money in big
chunks out of every paycheck, and resigned from my job at the end of
the year. I started a part-time private psychotherapy practice, and I
believe it was at this time that I began referring to myself publicly as a
feminist therapist. I also began teaching women's studies courses on
a part-time basis at local universities. I taught the introductory
women's studies course as well as Marriage and the Family, Psychology of Women, Women in Socialist Societies, a seminar on utopian
communal societies, especially looking at sex roles and the division
of labor, etc. I was also a member of the board of the Women's Studies
Program at Northeastern Illinois University.

In 1971, I heard Ann Tompkins, a social worker well-known to
those interested in Chinese-American relations, speaking and showing slides of the Peoples' Republic of China. She had lived there from
1965 to 1970, during the beginning of the Cultural Revolution. I was
thrilled and excited by what she said. Remembering fondly my journey to Cuba, I decided to find a way to go to China. I started speaking
about it to other members of the CWLU, and gradually a group of
women was formed. We started studying about China together and
wrote a proposal for our trip which we sent off to the Chinese embas-
sy in Ottawa, Canada, since this was before the Peoples' Republic of
China was diplomatically recognized by the United States. Then we
waited hopefully for a response. I knew it was possible for Americans to travel in China if they were sponsored by some kind of Chinese organization, since two friends of mine had gone on a tour of
Chinese factories and workplaces. During this process, President
Richard Nixon made his historic trip to China, and we all sat around
the television set, with our eyes glued to the screen, drinking in every
sight and every bit of information. We were finally invited to visit in
August, 1973, as guests of the China Travel organization, an "ordi-
nary friendship tour." This was not the time we had chosen, and we
had hoped to go as guests of the All-China Women's Federation.
Nevertheless, we eagerly said yes, we would go however we could.

While in China, we visited factories and other workplaces where
women were employed, health care facilities including an obstetri-

cal hospital, rural communes, museums, arts and crafts workshops, department stores, government organizations, etc. In every place, we met with the Revolutionary Committee in charge of the administration, and were told of the ever expanding role of women in the organization. Sometimes we were told of the heroic struggles of women to achieve equity in the workplace and in the political structure. Although Chinese government policy was "Equal work for equal pay," it was not so easily accomplished in face of thousands of years of patriarchal tradition. In addition to formal visits where we were accompanied by local guides as well as the two women translator/guides who accompanied us throughout the three week trip, we were able to use whatever little spare time we had (usually early morning or evening) to wander wherever we chose. We were also allowed to photograph almost every place we went, with the exception of the observation deck at one of the northern ports, and from the window of our airplane while traveling from one city to another. Our freedom to wander was limited only by our energy and our fluency with the language. Although I had studied Beijing dialect for about a year and a half before the trip, I found that it was still difficult for me to understand when Chinese was spoken. I was able to ask for simple things in the hotel with varying success, and attempt to converse with our local guides while riding in the tour bus or van, but did not feel confident in being able to find my way wandering the back streets of some of the most populous cities of the world. It was amazing, however, to be able to walk back to our hotel in Shanghai at 11 PM, and not feel danger in the dark streets.

The Chinese also felt that we had something to offer them. We had a long meeting with delegates from the municipal women's association. We had been asked to do a presentation on the U.S. women's liberation movement. It was felt that it was a heavy responsibility to represent all the women activists in this way, and we stayed up almost all night to prepare our various parts of the presentation.

One place that we repeatedly asked to go to on an official visit was the Shanghai Psychiatric Institute. Our Chinese hosts politely refused to comprehend why we would want to go to such a place unless it was to gawk at the freaks. We tried to explain that we had a psychologist, several social workers and a physician in our group, as well as others who were interested in a political comparison of their mental health system with the one in our country. I knew of other Americans who had visited the psychiatric facility. Finally, we were told that we would be unable to visit the Institute, but a meeting was arranged between us and some of the staff of the hospital. The meeting took place in the conference room on the top floor of our hotel and lasted several hours while we learned about the use of Chairman Mao's "little red book" as a basis for group therapy, in conjunction with acupuncture and the standard psychotropic medications with which we were familiar. There was often also intervention at the patient's workplace and in his home neighborhood. Clinical psychologists were not part of the treatment team, and were apparently unknown in that country.

When we returned to Chicago, we continued to be active as a collective. We thought about writing a book about our experience, and investigated the possibility with several publishers without success. We showed slides from our trip to almost any group that was interested, for a small fee, in order to earn money to pay back the loans made to several of our members for their travel expenses, our team taught courses on contemporary Chinese society at several local universities.

Twelve years later, in August, 1985, I had the opportunity to travel to China again. This time it was with a group of women psychologists from all over the country (and Canada), under the aegis of Division 35 (Psychology of Women) of the American Psychological Association. We were the guests of the Women's Association, and in Beijing stayed in their guest house, which had once belonged to the emperor. One of the women who had been our guide during our 1973 trip was now a director of the Women's Association. We again visited many interesting places, this time including Buddhist temples and famous Chinese rock gardens. I found that the introductory presentations at each site were not so thoroughly politicized now that the Great Proletarian Cultural Revolution was over—in contrast to when I had been there before. And, we were able to visit the Psychiatric Institute for a full tour this time! We presented papers at two conferences this time, having been asked to repeat them in a second city because we apparently made such a good impression in the first city. Our papers at the conferences were based on the research that had been done by feminist psychologists in the intervening time, and we covered topics we thought would be of interest to Chinese women. These included the effects on children of growing up in a one-child family and the dual career couple.

In 1982, the founding meeting of the Feminist Therapy Institute was held in Vail, Colorado, at the end of the ski season. Each of us attending had been encouraged to prepare a presentation. One of the papers presented was about multiple personality disorder and it set my head spinning because I began to think that one of my patients might fit that diagnosis. The prospect of working with such a patient provoked a great deal of anxiety in me, because it seemed so bizarre, and so difficult. My own paper was about the ethics of dual or over-lapping relationships. It was later expanded into a chapter in FTI's first book, *Handbook of Feminist therapy: Women's issues of psychothera-py* (1985). This led to another article on the same subject published in another book by FTI, *Feminist ethics in psychotherapy* (1991). Member-ship in FTI has kept me in touch with some of the most exciting women in feminist therapy, and has encouraged me to keep writing for publication, something not encouraged in my job as a clinician.

Among my recent activities has been participation in a task force working to re-write and promote state legislation criminalizing ther-apists' sexual exploitation of their clients. Although this issue was first brought to light as early as 1972, when Phyllis Chesler noted it in *Women and madness*, it continues to be a major factor in therapy, espe-cially in the therapy of women clients with male therapists.[1] This is a continued violation of basic trust between client and therapist. When women individually attempt to bring charges against perpe-trators they are often invalidated in ways similar to those used against other victims of sexual abuse and sexual assault.

Back in 1974, I was asked to participate in a Bachelor of Arts re-search project by answering a questionnaire (and being the natural archivist that I am, I saved a copy of my responses). At that time, my definition of feminist therapy was:

> Psychotherapy which integrates the concepts of the feminist movement (in my case, I would say the women's liberation movement), so that a woman can come to the understanding that many of the problems she faces in her life, and the unhappiness which brought her to seek therapy, are, at least to some extent, rooted in her socialization as a female, and in the oppression women experience in our society. Furthermore, the au-thoritarian role of the therapist is minimized. Optimally, it takes place in a group setting, where the client can get support from other women in making changes in her life. Women are *not* encouraged to adapt to tradi-tional female roles, but rather to make their own choices for the direction of their lives and assume control of their own lives.

As to whether or not a male therapist could be classified as a feminist therapist, I explained my negative answer in this way:

A male therapist can possibly help a woman to a certain point. However, because he lacks first-hand experience with what it is like to be a woman in our society, there are limits to his understanding and empathy. There are few, if any, men who are liberated from their socialized sex-roles and therefore continue to act towards women in oppressive ways, however subtle. Furthermore, a woman in therapy with a male, even with a raised consciousness of feminism, will usually continue to respond in a submissive and deferential way to male authority and paternalism.

I did not (and do not) think that feminist therapy is for women clients only, explaining that:

> While I prefer to work with women clients, there are some male clients whose concerns include overcoming the negative aspects of male socialization and sex-role stereotypes, and/or find themselves in conflict with the larger society's values and expectations for their behavior. Feminist therapy might be especially useful for male clients who identify themselves as gay or who are struggling with aspects of their sexual identity or the problems they encounter related to their sexual preference.

I found it difficult to answer with a simple "yes" or "no" the question of whether a feminist therapist could deal with male clients' problems adequately:

> "...On the one hand, to answer yes might seem a contradiction to what I have said about why a male therapist cannot be a feminist therapist, in terms of first hand life experience. On the other hand, it seems that it would depend on both the clients' goals and values and the therapist's orientation. For example, in terms of my answer the previous question, it seems possible that a feminist therapist is one which might most facilitate the growth of such a male client, while a male therapist might be threatened. Furthermore, there is a greater chance of competitiveness in a male–male relationship, hindering the process.

Finally, I distinguished between feminist therapy and humanistic therapy in this way:

> Humanistic therapy tends to emphasize intra-psychic processes and interpersonal interactions in the context of the individual, without consideration of the political and social environment. It ignores or avoids the processes and effects of socialization and economic and socio-cultural oppression. It does not make explicit the issues of feminism and does not raise the client's consciousness of these aspects of one's reality.

To these definitions, I would add that a feminist therapist is not an armchair practitioner and theoretician. She participates in activities which attempt to change and improve the society's treatment of and attitudes toward women and men.

In a recent newspaper column, Sally Quinn, a Washington, D.C. journalist, wrote that: "Women think the feminist movement is out of touch," and uses as examples Gloria Steinem, Jane Fonda, Barbra Streisand, and Patricia Ireland, a former president of NOW. She concluded by saying that, "The truth is that many women have come to see the feminist movement as anti-male, anti-child, anti-family, anti-feminine." What she says both angers and disappoints me. Sally Quinn is one of the women journalists who directly benefited from AWP's early media policy of speaking only to women reporters. I remember that she was one of those who covered the news of AWP's founding. It was the media that made people like Gloria Steinem a star, not the feminist movement. I never knew that Jane Fonda and Barbra Streisand were especially respected as women's movement activists. But more importantly, if it is true that women have come to see the feminist movement so negatively, it is because of the distorted and biased way it is still represented in the media, including television sit-coms and docu-dramas and male-directed movies from Hollywood. It is men who hate women and children, as evidenced by rape, woman battering, child sexual abuse, and forcing women and children into poverty by not paying child support. And yet many women are still male-identified because of the greater economic, social, and physical power men still have, after all these years. (It's been many years since Gordon Allport wrote about how the oppressed identify with the power of the dominant class or caste.) Rather than being anti-child and anti-family, it is the feminists who have raised the nation's awareness of issues of child abuse and woman abuse, and have founded shelters and rape crisis centers with many hours of volunteer sweat before municipal governments and the United Way decided to fund them. Feminism doesn't say women shouldn't have babies, but that they should have a choice about if and when to have them, and to have child- care centers and other social institutions to support their decisions and still be able to support their families. Feminism is, after all, about having the freedom to make choices—choices about whether to marry or not; choices about sexuality separate from reproduction; about whether to live a heterosexual, homosexual, bisexual or celibate life-style, choices about work; about education; about health care; and about safety. To some, these are still revolutionary ideas, and, thus, to some, feminist therapists are subversive!

NOTES

1. Ed's. note: Sexual contact with clients has been reported by from 9.4 % to 12.1% of licensed M.A. and Ph.D psychologists and 6.4% of psychiatrists. Reported by Pope, K. in THE AMERICAN PSYCHOLOGIST, July, 1988.

3

Looking Backward, Moving Forward

JEANNE ADLEMAN

"Good therapy builds toward authenticity, relatedness and strength, helps understand self and others as both sources of problems and resources for wellbeing . . . I am a well-aged former educator with wide-ranging life experience, twenty years as a counselor; am smart, flexible, intuitive, antiracist, well-respected, and love my work . . ." This is an excerpt from my self-description in a listing of therapists offering services. How did I get here from where I started?

I was born in 1919 into what I now describe as an urban (New York City) white-collar working class family, to highly Americanized Jewish parents with vaguely socialist ideals. My father died when I was six, and my mother's sister moved in with us so we could keep our apartment. Subsequently, my mother's half-sister separated from her husband and moved in too, with her three-year old daughter, providing me with a surrogate little sister and ending my only-child status. At times my mother's stepmother also lived with us, the only grandparent I ever knew. We lived in the Bensonhurst section of Brooklyn at a time when it was a Jewish and Italian community.

During the worst of the Depression years these three sisters managed to maintain the household their friends referred to as the house of women. Having lived their growing years in sometimes deep poverty, the sisters now told us children, "We're not *poor*, we're *broke*."

25

Certainly we were better off than millions of others, but it was sometimes hard for me to have not only a "real" mother but also two extra mothers.

In 1933 the entire household moved to Manhattan and I transferred from a co-ed to an all-female high school located near the College of the City of New York (CCNY). Between my apartment house and my high school stood Columbia University. Between our apartment and Columbia stood an excellent branch of the New York Public Library, where I rather randomly acquired a great deal of my book-learning.

Two years later, my mother married a gentle, kind man who had already become almost a part of the extended family. Now I had a father again and *we* three were a nuclear family as the sisters went their separate ways.

We were still economically marginal: my stepfather wrote adventure stories for pulp magazines that paid literally one cent a word. This enabled him to support himself, but my mother still supported herself and me on her Macy's salesclerk's salary. I did not yet understand my mother's desperate need to live in a middle-class building and neighborhood. Only years later did she tell me about the desolation of her growing years: poverty and insecurity; no place that could be called home; sleeping in other people's basements with her next-older sister and their probably crazy father; learning to visit the homes of better-off relatives at supper-time for one real meal of the day. All I "knew" was that 50% of their combined income went for housing, rather than the 25% maximum stipulated in my economics textbook. Consequently, we ate meat once a week, and lots of spaghetti the rest of the time, and I had to wear hand-me-down clothes. I also knew that the Depression still held sway, and that we were far from the most severely affected.

My mother lived in terror of losing her job, also true for most people who had jobs during those years of massive unemployment. This fear contributed to tensions at home. All three of us in this little family agreed quite well in our ideas about politics, but I was the only one who wanted to *do something* about injustice, inequality, threats of war or the Japanese invasion of Manchuria. I joined the National Student League because of its program to organize for racial equality, against fascism, and in support of workers' rights to organize into unions. During that year, the NSL merged with the Student League for Industrial Democracy to form the American Student Union. When I was elected president of my school's chapter of the

ASU I thought my leadership potential was being recognized, but in reality I was the only member not affiliated with either the Young Communist League or the Young People's Socialist League, therefore the only one the former rivals could agree on.

In April 1936 the ASU called for a national student strike for peace. Primarily based in colleges and universities, there were very few high school chapters but our small chapter took that strike seriously. The school administration's offer of a "peace assembly" turned out to be a set of red-baiting speeches, and we had no resources to meet outside the school, so we arranged to join with students at CCNY, who had a large chapter and had been able to secure the college's Great Hall for their meeting. Few experiences in my life have equaled the thrill of walking out the doors of our school, teachers required to enter the name of all 65 of us, "marching" a few blocks to the Great Hall, and being greeted by a roar of support from about 4,000 voices (all male at that time), ourselves feeling like heroes.

I was not yet seventeen years old, but was beginning to learn the power potential of even differing groups organized for common goals.

My punishment for this early activism was that I became a nonperson at my graduation ceremony in June 1936: prizes I had earned were not given to me, and the annual recognition of fifteen students for academic honors was reduced to ten (I would have been the eleventh). More important, my diploma was quietly withheld for awhile. Then my mother received a notice requiring her to appear with me at the giant bureaucracy known as The New York City Board of Education, to discuss the question of my diploma. I was more frightened of my mother than of the Board—hardly cared by then whether I ever got a diploma—but my timid mother was both angry and firm with the officials, and we left with my diploma in hand. Both of us had earned it. It had also cost her a day's pay.

Reflecting as I write this essay, I realize that part of her courage came from the depth of her intention that I get a college education. She wanted me to become a teacher as strongly as I wanted to become anything except a teacher—one more issue for us to battle over. To go to college, I would, of course, have to continue to live at home, attend one of the free colleges in New York, and work part-time. That Fall, I entered Brooklyn College as a student majoring in Political Science.

Conflicts at home continued to escalate, however. At the end of my first year I quietly began to seek full-time work and transferred to City College Evening Session's School of Education, the only area of

CCNY then accepting women students. Famously radical CCNY (the Evening Session being the most radical part of the school) introduced me to the term *male chauvinism*, what is now called sexism. Even then it was negative in principle but prevalent in practice.

Having read randomly in psychology at the Library, I was eventually able to register for my first real psychology *course*, Philosophy 5. As there was no psychology department at the time, psychology courses were taught within the Philosophy Department. Philosophy 5 was, I think, "Introduction to Psychology," taught by Isadore Chein whom I remember as a good and supportive teacher. As one part of the course we took psychological tests that we scored ourselves and then discussed. One was called a masculinity-femininity test. After scoring mine, I opened the discussion by saying furiously that this was not a masculinity-femininity test—it was a dominance-submission test. The year was no later than 1938, but I was already (at nineteen) angry at the idea that preferring to *follow* was called feminine; preferring to lead was masculine, along with willingness to voice opinions, and other healthy assertions I had learned to value.

During those years of college courses at night I discovered my ineptitude for retail sales. I took a crash course in shorthand and typing, and began working in offices. Verbal skills helped, and so did pretending to have graduated from college. I worked as a secretary, married, moved out of the city for a few years, dropped out of college, divorced, married someone else (who had two daughters from his first marriage) and with him had another daughter and a son; moved back to the city; kept on working as a secretary in various offices except for two years when I was pregnant or nursing and tried freelance writing (with no success).

Secretary was my job, but never my identity. My identity was political organizer, an activity that took place in my so-called free time. Sometimes I was fortunate enough to earn my living at work that advanced my politics, but that was a rare privilege.

I might still be a secretary by day and a radical organizer by night if history had not taken some major turns in the mid-fifties. Leaders died and their successors began to tell people in each country how those leaders had lied. Parties of what is now called the Old Left, in the U.S. as elsewhere in the world, fell into disarray. Refusing to trust people who said they had lied to us but were now telling the truth, I no longer had a political base from which to organize. But if I were not a political organizer what identity would I have?

Some things I thought I could trust: civil disobedience for civil and human rights; children's search for learning, growth, and truths they could rely on. Maybe I would be a teacher after all. I also wanted a job where I would earn the same salary as a man doing the same job. When I left my last full-time secretarial job I was replaced by two men, each earning more when they started than I was earning after five years.

I re-entered Brooklyn College at age 38 as a Junior, still working full-time and going to classes at night. In my final year I had to be in school full-time to complete the seminar on elementary school curriculum, fulfill the student-teaching practicum, and make up any missing requirements such as music for elementary school teachers and a laboratory science. At last I graduated in 1960, Cum Laude, with Honors in Education.

Having student-taught at two different levels in each of two elementary schools, having been a star student-teacher, I felt ready to take on my own classroom. I couldn't have been more mistaken. Like most beginning teachers, in New York City, perhaps especially, I found myself resorting to teacher behaviors I had vowed never to exhibit: yelling, threatening, manipulating, and worst of all, sometimes humiliating children (not always intentionally). I hated myself and the system, myself more. What saved my sanity was the support that came from those very same old-timers, the traditional teachers, the women derided as "old biddies" by the sophisticated public and academic critics, who would tell me my class was "improving so much"; or that I had "done wonders" with a well-known "problem child."

Between 1960 and 1970 I taught in three different Brooklyn schools (second, third, and sixth grade classes); was invited back to Brooklyn College to teach Elementary Education and refused because I was only just learning how to teach; in 1962 moved to Manhattan where I lucked into a school with an extraordinary principal (Edward P. Gottlieb) who appreciated and strengthened everything innovative and supportive I wanted to do—including teaching certain skills to children in sixth grade: self-evaluation, critical thinking, discussion, and negotiation. When I was again invited back to Brooklyn College (still with only a B.A.) I accepted and spent two years there on leave from the Board of Education to the Board of Higher Education; returned with relief in 1967 to elementary school teaching; confronted my husband on certain issues, a confrontation that led to our separation and eventual divorce; survived for a while the retirement of the wonderful principal; earned a Masters degree in Teacher Education at Columbia University Teacher College; got involved as a teacher-community liaison in the local antipoverty agency (which was simultaneously frustrating and rewarding); and saw my children off to begin their independent lives.

I continued to love teaching the resistant, rebellious children, but ultimately could not survive the new principal. He was about to reassign me out of my classroom and into an alternate position because I refused to adopt his pet reading program. I left in midyear in a rage at him and in tears at leaving the class. I made plans to leave New York City and experiment with living on the West Coast.

Once again, however, as in the mid-fifties, other forces were at work. At Fordham University in the Bronx (New York) there was an experimental college, Bensalem, founded in 1967 by Elizabeth Sewell (a Fordham faculty member) with the support of Father Leo McLoughlan, then president of the University. Elizabeth Sewell had hoped to create a college modeled after Oxford University in England, with resident faculty, small seminar courses, and tutorials, but the rebellious and countercultural politics of young American students carried the autonomy of the College's charter into decidedly non-Oxford pathways.

In one of the more productive projects, several Bensalem students, with one faculty member and an adjunct, had responded to a New York City teachers' strike by forming an alternative "free school" for children, the Bensalem students as teachers. The school continued after the strike ended, and several students decided on teaching as their career. Now, in 1970, the involved Bensalem faculty planned to leave and the search was on for someone who could develop a teacher-preparation program to submit to the State Department of Education for provisional accreditation. I did not have a Ph.D. but I did have that Masters in Teacher Education, and they hired me.

Between 1970 and 1977 I lived through some transformative experiences—many at the same time; three years with Bensalem students, a move to San Francisco, another year at a different alternative undergraduate college, two years at a Montessori school, completion of the training program at the Gestalt Institute of San Francisco, and more.

The Bensalem years were exhilarating, tumultuous, maddening, full of failures and successes, an experience I still hope to document some day. With the processes we developed, each student who applied to the State did receive a provisional license. Fordham phased out Bensalem by June, 1974.

In San Francisco I had a one-year, half-time appointment at one of the "University Without Walls" programs that sprang up in the early 1970s. Again, with students, I developed an alternative teacher-preparation program, provisionally accredited by California. Subsequently I worked as adjunct (tutorial) faculty with students in Goddard College's Field Experience M.A. program.

During one enlightening three-month period I volunteered with the collective that published *Issues in Radical Therapy,* whose motto, "Therapy is change, not adjustment," had inspired me to think maybe some day I could be a therapist. I could not continue with that collective, however, because I was too busy with my next job as Administrator of a parent-and-staff-owned Montessori school adapted to the mores of a diverse set of teachers and parents. I absolutely loved that job and thought I was making a worthy contribution both to the school and to the independent school community.

Toward the end of my first year, the parent who chaired the Board of Directors approached me to ask which parents I would like to have on next year's Board. I answered that I didn't think it was appropriate for the Administrator to select the Board members. I still think my ethics in that situation were correct, but my response may have proved my undoing because at the end of the second year the new Board made plain that they did not want to renew their (verbal) contract with me.

57 years old, I was no longer an enthusiastic educator with pride in myself and in our school but unemployed, rootless, disheartened and sometimes near-suicidal. I did not see how I could motivate myself back into the job market at that age. 'Though I had completed Gestalt training by then, I did not feel ready to become a therapist. I lived minimally for most of a year, on unemployment insurance interspersed with occasional temporary administrative jobs offered by people who knew me or knew of me.

Even before 1970, but especially during this seven-year period, a consciousness I was not ready to call "feminist" kept growing in me. Challenged by my daughters I responded: "If every woman of every social class were to achieve complete equality with every man of that same class, there would still be massive injustice and inequality in the world." Nevertheless, one day I experienced the famous *click!* and added, "Of course there is no way that that can happen without massive changes in society as a whole." I began to pay serious attention to writings and actions coming out of women's movement organizations. Still, I could hardly think the word "feminist" without the preface, "bourgeois."

In the miserable period from 1976 to 1977 I volunteered in some women's organizations which helped my morale by valuing my skills and experience while encouraging me to value myself a little more, even my potential as a therapist (which had also been encouraged by some of the faculty at the Gestalt Institute). I was also meeting and working for the first time with numbers of lesbians, most of whom seemed thoughtful, bold, full of initiative and completely dedicated to women's lives, wants and needs.

By the summer of 1977 I began to list myself in alternative directories not as a therapist but as a "Resource for personal strength and social solidarity." When I did begin to identify myself as a therapist those words still described what I aimed to provide. I no longer considered suicide. I moved slowly but increasingly in the direction of considering myself a feminist therapist. Feminist therapy has been variously defined, often as "an educative modality," meaning that there is nothing wrong with sometimes simply teaching clients something we have reason to believe we know that they seem not to know. To do this respectfully and responsibly is not easy, yet it can be done. How I evolved as a therapist grew almost organically from the sensitivities I had learned as a teacher and especially as a supervisor of student teachers.

Among other interests I have routinely monitored my dreams since my experience in Jungian analysis in the 1940s. In the course of Gestalt training I discovered that I had some special aptitude for facilitating client dreamwork in the drop-in groups. Later I found imaginative and successful ways of linking the group and the individual, while resisting interpretation and projection by others, and maintaining the client as the only expert on her or his dream's significance. Those who supervised me during that period considered me skillful and approved of my work. I greatly preferred Gestalt dreamwork to what I had experienced in Jungian analysis, though I have only appreciation for the analyst who worked with me for two years the first time around, and another year later on.

Unconsciously, I now realize, I modeled myself on that analyst as I began to have clients. Her name was Martha Jaeger. She was of Quaker origin; a student of Zen more than fifty years ago; had trained at the Jung Institute in Switzerland and had had her didactic analysis with Otto Rank. None of this applies to me, yet I know I have adopted many of her modes of practice and ways of being, though I never followed her orientation.

In 1980 I entered what was called a Mentorship Program in Existential Humanistic Psychology, and for two trimesters was part of a small group studying and working with James F. T. Bugental; this was another important step in my development. I wish I could say the same about the two *years* I spent at a fee-supported graduate school that accepted me in 1981. My first year there was a happy one. I thrived on my classes and on the readings, including Statistics; liked all but one of my instructors; wrote papers I can reread with satisfaction still; challenged male-supremacist psychologies, and received interesting and useful evaluations. I especially appreciated the students I met there, and my freedom to think critically and speak my thoughts.

During the second year most of that drained away. There were only two worthwhile experiences: one, I taught a full-credit course on women's issues in psychotherapy; two, I was elected Student Representative to the school's Board of Directors where I learned enough to keep me skeptical about its vaunted social change commitments. For the rest of my five thousand dollars' worth I was required to take courses called Psychopathology and Adult Assessment, Psychology of the Borderline, etc., the content of which violated most of my principles. I left at the end of the second year owing thousands of dollars in student loans plus 9% interest, glad to have given myself the chance, glad to have learned some of what I had learned, and enormously relieved to be quit of the school.

In 1980 I had attended a conference of the Association for Women in Psychology, and immediately joined. In 1983 I attended the second national meeting of the Feminist Therapy Institute, in Washington, D.C. Sixty of us raced through abbreviated presentations of papers we received to take home. At that meeting, the Institute became a membership organization, and I, one of the members.

Near the end of the weekend, someone had to volunteer to organize the 1984 meeting. Lauree Moss said she would do it if I would work with her. Sara Sharratt and Lilian Bern volunteered to be part of an organizing committee and the group gave us the authority. The work built slowly throughout the ensuing year, and—I was de facto almost an insider. Involvement with The Feminist Therapy Institute, Inc., initially helped me leave the doctoral program (I found that in feminist circles I didn't need a doctorate for my thinking, speaking and writing to be appreciated). In the course of the next several years, during which I was on FTI's Steering Committee and attended every annual meeting, members seemed to value me as an interesting and provocative thinker, speaker and writer. Whereas I had felt under assault during my second year in the doctoral program, here I could grow again and continue my development. Had it not been for FTI, I doubt if I would ever have been able, with Gloria Enguídanos, to co-edit a recently published book titled *Racism in the Lives of Women: Testimony, theory, and guides to antiracist practice*.

FTI, like AWP, and like many women's liberation movements everywhere, pointed up how individual, group and academic psychology is inescapably interconnected with politics and society. Class is one issue that was frequently brought up for consciousness-raising but was originally perceived by some FTI members as excessively critical and divisive. Race is another.

The 1986 annual meeting of FTI erupted after two participants criticized others for racist comments or racism in their papers or discussions. Most of us white women did not immediately know how to respond. Nan Jervey deserves credit for following up after the meeting; she prodded me to join her in creating a response to the need. Together we asked the Chair to establish an antiracism committee. She responded by creating a "Diversity Task Force." A year later the Steering Committee voted it into full status as FTI's Antiracism Committee, which has functioned ever since. Committees and good intentions do not, of course, resolve the distances and guardedness of people, even or especially feminists, on all sides of such a profound issue.

Class and racial equality issues have been among my lifelong concerns and I am grateful to the working-class women and people of color (as well as some white and middle-to-upper-class women) who insist that the issues remain in the forefront of feminist attention, despite our many other agendas.

And what about Jewish women, what about anti-Semitism? Are we, as more than one woman has said to me, *merely* "generic white women" rather than targets of discrimination, cruelty and hate? What about all the other so-called minorities? These are some of the tasks on contemporary feminist agendas.

Both AWP and FTI appeared to me to be "homes" equally for lesbian, bisexual and heterosexual women; nevertheless, painfully heated tensions sometimes arose among us. I experienced these tensions from within my still-new identity as a lesbian. Way back in my teen years I knew I was sexually attracted to both girls and boys—it was what drove me to the public library psychology shelves to try to understand myself. From what I read I derived a belief that I could accept these attractions but that eventually I would find myself heterosexual and thus a real woman. In 1975, at 56, I made a quarter-turn in my sexual orientation by deciding it was time at last to fully explore bisexuality. A bisexual life is clearly right for some, but for me it was unsatisfactory at many levels. I began to wonder if I could perhaps make the turn all the way to lesbianism. In 1980, with the help of a therapist, I concluded that I could, and I did. I made a commitment to live the rest of my life as a lesbian. It is fifteen years later as I write, and I have never been sorry. I am where I wanted and want to be.

There are many feminist therapists today who have entered the field of feminist therapy through doors of social/political activism and advocacy especially on women's issues. As many or more had traditional—sometimes known as male-model or medical-model—professional training. These usually, but not necessarily, more privileged women frequently became feminist therapists as a result of their personal experiences of discrimination, harassment and abuse in academic or clinical settings. I have been both fascinated by and appreciative of the ways that women of diverse backgrounds have worked together toward increasing professionalization of Feminist Therapy. Such professionalism, and the collaborative nature of FTI's work toward it, is evident in the Feminist Therapy Code of Ethics (copy available from Polly Taylor, FTI Administrator, 904 Irving St. #258, San Francisco, CA 94122).

Sometimes I miss the early days and years—the raggedy, boisterous, know-it-all, risky and heady sense of being pioneers, even the anti-psychiatry movement. I am neither cynical nor jaded when I speak for a professionalism grounded minimally in diagnostics and expertise, maximally in accountability, accountability not to the state or the law so much as to the human beings for (and sometimes upon) whom we practice. I believe we are also accountable to each other if we claim to be feminists. Food for learning grows everywhere and nourishes minds that keep open.

II

FEMINIST THERAPISTS AND THEIR ORGANIZATIONS

4

Going Around in Circles and Coming Out in the Same Place and Different Places— My Development As a Feminist Therapist

BARBARA E. SANG

The invitation to write about my experience as a feminist therapist came at the right time in my life. As a mid-life woman, born in 1937, these past 13 years have been a period of reflection, and a pulling together of various parts of my life. I welcomed another opportunity to continue this process. Interest in my own midlife issues led me to research this area and to collaborate with two other midlife colleagues—Joyce Warshow and Adrienne Smith. We have just finished co-editing an anthology entitled, *Lesbians at Midlife—the Creative Transition.* (1)

As far as I can remember, I have always been different. As a child growing up in New York City, I stood out from my peers by being considerably smaller and thinner and by wearing home-made clothes, as opposed to store-bought clothes. Although I was a bright artistic person, school was a disaster. This was because, unbeknownst to me at the time, I was severely dyslexic. I had difficulty with reading and with written expression. Dyslexia also affected me in many other areas. I took my frustration out by being a "tom boy" and could generally be found sitting high on top of some tree.

I did better in high school than grade school but my performance continued to be extremely uneven. Nonetheless, for a teenager of that time period, I had serious intellectual interests. While my female classmates were absorbed in making themselves physically attractive to boys, I was reading a great deal, making art, attending concerts and theater and playing several musical instruments. I had even joined a political club and was the only female. None of my girlfriends shared my interests and I often felt lonely and like an outsider. My adolescence was spent trying to figure out what my career was going to be. I would have liked to have been a naturalist or a biologist but my difficulty with numbers discouraged me from these fields. Therefore, I decided to be an artist.

When it came time for me to go to college I was dissuaded from doing so, not only because females in the 1950's were not supposed to take themselves seriously, but because I was not a good student in the conventional sense. I deliberately picked a college that valued creative thinking over traditional academic achievement. This was a good choice because an alternative education brought out my strengths. Considering the time period, Bard College was one of the few schools where women were taken as seriously as men. I switched my major from art to psychology—a field that enabled me to combine both my interests in art and science. Bard was not without its problems, one of which was its sexual permissiveness. Once again, I felt different because I was not having affairs with the opposite sex. I did try to be like everyone else but it did not feel right.

I sought out psychotherapy at this time because I was worried about my sexual orientation. My therapist assured me that once I worked out my problems this "symptom" would disappear. She also questioned why a nice college girl like myself would want to have Modigliani prints on her wall instead of football pennants like other (normal?) college students. Eventually I changed therapists.

A person who had considerable impact on my development during this time was my second therapist—a psychiatrist in her early forties named Irma Gross Drooz. Irma had a specialty in neurology and had wanted to be a brain surgeon but, as she put it, "Who in their right mind would entrust their brains to a woman?" She settled for psychiatry. We had an exceptionally close and trusting relationship that enabled me to work through many of my problems. I also got support for wanting to have a career. Irma realized that I had much untapped potential and her confidence in me enabled me to take risks and to function with more self confidence.

Back in the 50's it was an uncontested rule that therapists did not divulge their personal lives. What I appreciated most about my work with Irma was her openness and willingness to reveal her personal experiences. Such sharing gave me a glimpse into the life of an adult who had her own problems and conflicts. We talked a lot about the fact that our relationship did not fit the books and about our own client/therapist process. I felt I benefited greatly from her flexibility and humanness and have found discretionary self-disclosure to be therapeutic in my own practice. Tragically, Irma died of Hepatitis B in her late forties while I was on my clinical internship in Washington, D.C. At least she knew I was on my way to becoming a professional. I owe my success to her skill. She was clearly a feminist before her time.

It all began in the mid-60's when I was trying to "come out" as a lesbian. While doing my research internship at St. Elizabeths Hospital in Washington, D.C., I would sneak away from my work to the stacks and read books on women and homosexuals. Such writers as Helene Deutsch and Simone de Beauvoir portrayed women and lesbians in such a negative and stereotyped way I knew that something was wrong. Shortly afterward, I joined the Daughters of Bilitis, a lesbian organization in New York, to meet other women like myself. I quickly became the education chairperson and led discussions on lesbian lifestyles and brought in speakers. The lesbians I met did not fit the stereotype of those portrayed in the psychology literature. Since I am the kind of person who doesn't accept things as they are, I set out to learn everything I could about lesbianism. I presented a paper at one of the very first panels (1975) at the American Psychological Association's annual convention had on homosexuality. My non-traditional education prepared me to challenge what I didn't agree with.

The women's movement was just becoming strong in the mid to late 60's and it spoke to me. I became involved in NOW and a women's CR group. It was reassuring to meet other women who shared the same values as myself. Had the women's movement not taken up all my energies, I might have gone on for advanced training at one of the analytic institutes. With my new feminist consciousness however, I realized I didn't belong in a traditional institute that was sexist, racist, classist and homophobic. I said to myself, "Why get trained to work in a way that you would be fighting to free yourself of?" I felt we as women needed to have a fresh start—to be open—to have "no mind" (to use a Zen concept.)

From the beginning it has always been my belief that you can't make existing models of personality and development non-sexist by changing a few words or the meaning of certain words. These models are "world views" which determine the way you describe (diagnoses) a person, the questions you ask or don't ask and the interpretations you make. I felt we needed our own theories and models and that could only come about if we let go of the old thinking and did our best to be true to our own perceptions and experience. In 1971 I wrote a position paper entitled: "*What is a feminist therapist?* for a NOW publication called *Now and Then* (2). In addition to acknowledging how rigidly-defined sex roles oppress women, I stressed the importance of the language we used to talk about ourselves. Such terms as "penis envy" and "masculine woman", have sexist connotations. My own approach was to describe what I saw in descriptive terms.

A former classmate and colleague, Lila Lowenberg, and I met once a week for several years to develop non-sexist ways of working with clients. We believed that what made our approach feminist was not just the content of what was dealt with, or our social awareness, but the assumptions underlying the way in which we did therapy. For example, one characteristic of our process was to do away with polarized thinking and relating—a way of experiencing the self and others in a dichotomous, judgmental manner. We can prevent polarized positions from forming when we can validate someone else's point of view while simultaneously maintaining the validity of our own point of view. If we believe that our way is the only way we oppress the other person. We were concerned about helping our clients and ourselves to define differences in personal style without resorting to judgmental labels. Also, by labeling certain qualities as "masculine" or "feminine" we perpetuate sex role stereotypes. We suggested describing a particular quality without qualifying it as to gender. Lila and I had planned to write a book but it never materialized. We did write several position papers.

For many years almost all the books I read, the lecturers, workshops and conferences I attended were by feminists, lesbians and gay males. I could no longer read the traditional literature which was based on the assumption that anyone not interested in relating to the opposite sex or desirous of children was not "normal". Women who were assertive and career-oriented were considered "disturbed". I began to question what other assumptions these theories were making about healthy development and I found much that did not fit my experience. My own philosophy of development grew out of my own observations with women, lesbians and gay males.

In 1971 I attended the very first homophile conference at Rutgers University and met Ralph Blair, a counseling psychologist. We both strongly felt that homosexual individuals needed the kind of counseling and therapy in which there was a real option to be themselves. Gay people needed therapists attuned to their unique issues such as "coming out" or raising children. Out of the need to provide the gay community with positive therapy services, The Homosexual Community Counseling Center (HCCC), one of the first alternative counseling centers in this country, was formed. (It is still in existence.) The HCCC provided me with the opportunity of working with a diverse population of lesbians with whom I would otherwise not have had contact. These women were from various socio-economic backgrounds, racial and ethnic groups and of all different ages.

Based on my experience with a large number of lesbians I found the views expressed in the mental health literature on lesbians to be inaccurate. In fact, as the criteria of mental health for women began to change, lesbians were often found to be more self-realized because they were not constrained by conventional social roles! In 1977 my paper, "*Psychotherapy with lesbians: Some observations and tentative generalizations* (3) was the first of its kind to be included in an anthology on psychotherapy and women and to be published by a major publishing company. In that article I outlined some of the problems that lesbians brought to therapy and how traditional therapists tended to pathologize what they heard rather than viewing lesbians within a social context.

In 1972, Susanne Schad-Somers, a sociologist and psychotherapist who was on the board of the Homosexual Community Counseling Center, came to me and said, "Let's do for all women what we are doing for homosexuals." I agreed and the Women's Psychotherapy Referral Service came into being. Therapists were admitted to the service on the basis of their feminist consciousness and political participation in the women's movement. One's view on homosexuality was also an important screening device. At this time I was an active

member of NOW New York and was getting numerous requests for
therapists who were sympathetic to women's issues. Many feminists were finding their therapists to be sexist and were no longer
able to work with them. There was clearly a need to make therapists
with non-sexist biases available to the public. It seemed natural for
the new women's service to be affiliated with NOW. In other cities at
this time women's psychotherapy services were connected with
NOW. The New York NOW board, however, felt that such a liaison
would be self-serving, ie: that we would be perceived as endorsed by
NOW and receive clients from them when they would rather not be
seen as "giving" us clients. As a result of my battle with NOW over
affiliation, plus the fact that case presentations within our group did
not seem much different from conventional groups, I felt frustrated
and I resigned. I had been hoping to work with women who were
looking to create a new model—a new process and whose primary
identification was not with the orientation of their training. I didn't
have the foresight to realize that a feminist psychology needed time
to develop.

Back in the mid 70's there still was not that much that had been
written on the psychology of women. I realized this when I was putting together my feminist psychology course for Sagaris, a school for
independent political thought, in 1975. Phyllis Chesler's *Women and
Madness* (4) and Barbara Ehrenreich's and Deirdre English's book
Complaints and Disorders—The Sexual Politics of Sickness (5) were my
main texts. A year later Elizabeth Friar Williams' *Notes of a Feminist
Therapist* (6) was in print and it pulled together much of the common
knowledge that was developing. For years this remained the only
book where feminist therapy issues were explored.

During the '70's the most radical position papers presenting alternative therapy models for women were being circulated around by a
network of women who shared similar values. These papers became
my main source of stimulation and inspiration. Most of the papers
were never published or, if they were, it was in an obscure publication. An example of such a paper is, *My assumptions in doing feminist
consultation* by Dorothy Riddle (7). JoAnn Gardner, a psychologist
and prominent feminist activist, operated her own press out of Pittsburgh—Know Inc. where one could send for reprints of published
and unpublished position papers. Another important source of support for me at that time was contact with a few select colleagues who
were challenging the system. My former classmate and friend, Ro-
byn Posin, moved to California in the mid '70's. Ever since, we have

corresponded on women's issues and on our own personal experiences as lesbian women and psychotherapists.

After resigning from the Women's Psychotherapy Referral Service I connected with Betty Kronsky, a former member of the service, who had also just resigned. We discovered that we were both interested in the creative process and after much negotiation, the Artist Therapy Service (ATS) was launched with six other individuals (3 women, 3 men). This was the first time that I had worked with men for many years. I felt ready to collaborate with others who did not necessarily share my views. Around this period I found myself feeling bored with what was going on in feminist psychology. The Association for Women in Psychology seemed to be made up of mostly students who, as yet, had not practiced psychotherapy. I longed to be with more experienced peers. ATS served this function. My own interest was in women and the creative process and I published one of the first papers in this area (1981) in a journal called *The Arts and Psychotherapy*(7). I was also using my feminist consciousness to develop more effective ways of working in psychotherapy with women artists. I have recently published an article on the subject (9).

In the late '70's to mid '80's I felt the need to be more reflective and less politically active. I also felt the need to focus more on my own creative expression, i.e. art. My reading at this time was mainly oriental philosophy and alternative forms of healing which ultimately got integrated into my approach to psychotherapy. I was writing articles on *"Zen, creativity and psychotherapy* (10), *The joy of creativity* (11), and *Art as healing* (12).

During this period I felt something was missing. I went back to some of my old books by Karen Horney, Harry Stack Sullivan, Erich Fromm and Melanie Klein and looked at them from my new feminist perspective. I found I could still learn something from them but this was not what I was looking for. Some of the existential writers, whom I had just begun to read, such as Anthony Storr, James Bugental, Irvin Yalom and Frances Vaughan felt more compatible with my own experience; I have incorporated some of their ideas into my own feminist process. As my reading became more broadly based, I realized that there were many books on women that had little or no feminist consciousness. A case in point is *Women Treating Women* (13) by Bernstein & Warner.

In 1985 I joined the steering committee of the NOW National Conference in New York, and as a result of the inspiring leadership of Doris Howard, one of the contributors to this book, I once again became more active in the organization. In recent years there have been so many good books and journals on women's psychology it is hard to keep up with them. There is a lot to learn and the field is becoming more specialized. I look back on the days when I knew everything that was going on. Since I am a very slow reader it feels particularly overwhelming.

My definition of a feminist therapist is a complex one and this does not feel like the place to do it justice. Nevertheless, let me say a little on the subject. My role as a therapist is a multiple one: I am a facilitator, teacher, consciousness raiser, information provider, role model, translator, etc. Therapy involves enabling (through facilitation) a person to be who they are rather than who they should be as defined by others and society. It involves helping a person to make choices and feel in control of her or his life. Each person's life is an adaptation that makes sense. By my validating where a person is in their life it frees that person to remain the same or to change. We grow if we have options. If we are forced to defend our position we can get caught in that and don't have the freedom or energy to see other possibilities. Part of this process involves helping an individual get in touch with her or his feelings, needs and values.

I use myself differently with each client, depending on their needs and issues. Psychotherapy is similar to improvisation and it requires the therapist to be open and creative. With artists, particularly women, I have found it therapeutic to attend art shows, concerts, theater performances, etc. and have written about my rationale for doing so in my paper on psychotherapy with women artists. (No, I don't attend weddings!) Like most feminist therapists I am also concerned with the power dynamics between client and therapist.

We live in a society that values instant change without having to go through the hard work that is necessary to make it happen. It is easy to forget that psychotherapy is about a relationship between two people which takes time to develop. I don't routinely use some of the more currently popular techniques such as imaging, visualization, and meditation, but if they are introduced by the client, or they arise spontaneously, they can be useful. I am concerned about the current trend in self-help groups which supply people with a ready made vocabulary to talk about their feelings. I find clients tend to adopt these convenient labels and are sometimes reluctant to explore what a particular experience means to them. Not only are many of these labels sexist because they put the blame on women, but they alienate women from their own authentic voice.

I have noticed some changes in my practice over the years. More women are concerned with working on themselves and are placing less emphasis on their relationships. For some reason I am seeing more women who have difficulty expressing their thoughts and feelings. By this point in time I would have thought that younger women would be less oppressed by stereotypical notions of femininity but this is not the case. For example, one client who grew up athletic feels comfortable wearing casual clothes. However, she worries about whether the opposite sex will find her attractive because she is not "feminine enough". An increasing number of women are in positions with considerable responsibility and overtime work. These women have little time for leisure, are stressed and are not taking care of themselves. We are also experiencing a backlash: younger women are feeling pressured to get married and have children.

During the last five years or so things have come together for me. After twelve years, I have rejoined the Women's Psychotherapy Referral Service. While most of the women don't have as their goal the creation of a new feminist model, this does not upset me as it did in the past. I find that each woman in the group has her own unique contribution and I can learn from it. I have joined the Feminist Therapy Institute which has more women who share my views. Although I can't afford to attend yearly meetings, I still feel connected. As metro New York coordinator for the Association for Women in Psychology I have organized several stimulating discussion groups which have been a good learning experience for me. The women in the Artist Therapy Service (ATS) seceded from the men because they got tired of doing their chores and taking care of them emotionally. At present I have been working on developing more effective ways of working with women artists.

I also belong to a women's peer supervision group that meets monthly and find our process to be invaluable. Sometimes just getting such feedback as I am working too hard is quite helpful.

My most gratifying source of communication and stimulation continues to be with a few select friends and colleagues. Between these personal interchanges, my group affiliations, occasional supervision of doctoral dissertations, reading and my own writing, my professional life feels full. Once in a while I venture out into the mainstream world to attend something that touches on my own interests. Most recently, I attended the thirty-seventh annual Karen Horney lecture given by Joyce McDougall—"Femininity and creativity: their relationship to the personal construct of sexual identity." The talk consisted of a case presentation of a lesbian writer who allegedly was blocked in her work. Both father's creative penis and mother's womb were said to be necessary for creativity; she lacked the father's input. Despite the fact that McDougall's client was in a relationship with another woman, the focus was on her relationships with men. McDougall views homosexuality as a "perversion". This talk gave me the feeling I was back in the 1950's again. The audience was made up almost entirely of women. The first person to be called on was a man who, wouldn't you know it, asked, "Did the analysis cure her of her homosexuality?" I have attended other similar talks given by analytic institutes over the years, and have found the way in which women and lesbians are discussed to be alienating.

Many of the areas that feminists deal with have tended to be about women as victims, e.g., rape, incest and women battering. It is important that we continue to work to eradicate such violence against women. However, we also need to develop a psychology that includes the other side of women's experience such as joy, play, healthy pride, creativity and spirituality. I also believe that a feminist perspective can be used to explore areas we don't usually associate with a psychology of women. As a dyslexic woman, I realized how many of the characteristics of dyslexia were what women were trained to be, i.e., helpless, flighty and apologetic. From my experience working with clients who were dyslexic, it became apparent that therapists did not realize they were working with a dyslexic female because her behavior could be explained by other factors. I wrote a paper, On being female and dyslexic which was published in the Journal, *Women and Therapy.*

I would like to conclude this paper with the following observation: Unlike most systems and models of psychotherapy, feminist therapy is unique in that it is based on the views of many individuals—not just one individual. I hope that a feminist analysis of therapy remains an open system and that as we move along, we can modify it and change it as the world changes and we have more input from women of different races and backgrounds. I hope that feminist theory never becomes another ism or a rigid dogma but rather continues to be an open-ended dialogue that can incorporate new views and continues to be flexible and sensitive. At the present time most of the training that is available to feminist women is of a traditional nature. Perhaps some day there will be training institutes that teach existing theories as historical background but which focus on some of the new feminist ways of thinking about and working with clients.

REFERENCES

1. Sang, B., Warshow, J, & Smith, A. (Eds.) *Lesbians at Midlife: The Creative Transition.* San Francisco: Spinster Book Co. 1991.
2. Sang, B. What is a feminist therapist? *Now and Then.* New York: National Organization for Women Newsletter. 1971.
3. Sang, B. Psychotherapy with lesbians; Some observations and tentative generalizations. In E. Rawlings & D. Carter (Eds.) *Psychotherapy for Women: Treatment Towards Equality.* Springfield, Il: Charles C. Thomas. 1977. pp. 266–75.
4. Chesler, P. *Women and Madness.* New York: Doubleday.1972.
5. Ehrenreich, B. & English, D. *Complaints and Disorders: The Sexual Politics of Sickness.* New York. The Feminist Press. 1973.
6. Williams, E. F. *Notes of a Feminist Therapist.* New York: Praeger Publishers. 1976.
7. Riddle, D. My assumptions in doing feminist consultation. Unpublished paper. 1975.
8. Sang, B. Women and the creative process. *The Arts in Psychotherapy.* 8. 1981. pp. 43–48.
9. Sang, B. Psychotherapy with women artists. *The Arts in psychotherapy.* 16. 1989. pp. 301–307.
10. Sang, B. Zen, creativity and psychotherapy. Paper presented as part of the Artists' Therapy Service Spring Series, Soho 20 Gallery. 1984.
11. Sang, B. The joy of creativity. Unpublished paper. 1986.
12. Sang, B. Integrating the emotional, spiritual, social and athletic parts of myself through nature photography. Paper presented at the Artists' Therapy Service program: Art as Healing. 1983.
13. Bernstein, A. & Warner, G. *Women Treating Women.* New York: International Universities Press. 1984.
14. Sang, B. On being female and dyslexic. *Women and Therapy.* 7. pp. 15–34. 1988.

5

Finding a Home in Feminist Therapy

DORIS HOWARD

My development as a feminist began within my family. Born in 1927, I grew up at a time when gender restrictions were very powerful but there were some equally powerful influences stemming from members of my own family. It was my good fortune to have many women on both sides of my family who did not fall into traditional family roles. For example, several of my aunts chose not to have children. Their reasons may have been religious, age-related or personal but at least I observed that they had a choice. From everything that I observed in the family legends, I was preceded by some very strong women. Not least among them, whatever her other characteristics, was my mother. She was orphaned at an early age, along with a younger sister and brother, and was in the care of a very strong grandmother. My mother had an 8th grade education and began working some time in her teens. I have heard that she was a personable young woman who was outgoing, fun-loving, and devoted to hard work. When I was a child she often told me with pride that she had worked up to the level of factory forelady who actually supervised men—this in the second decade of this century! She definitely taught me, by example, that women could and did enjoy having careers. She also gave me the impression that she was sorry to give it up at age 36, when she married and started a family.

My interest in therapy seems to me to have been lifelong. I had one particularly glamorous aunt who had an interesting career in the music-publishing business. I heard for years that she was "in analysis." (I shudder to think what this meant in the 1930's.) I was a rather depressed and frightened child and was fascinated by the idea of "analysis." When my father died, when I was 13, the die was cast. I could not understand life at all. When I look back, my life from age 13 to age 30 was a yellow-brick-path leading toward my first consultation. After beginning interpersonal (Sullivanian) analysis, I was consumed by the idea of becoming a therapist, myself, although it was years before I had the courage to articulate that to others. I can clearly recall, as early as age 5, thinking about my life and wondering why things were as they were. Puzzles were interesting to me. Later, in midlife, I realized there were three potential careers that had excited my early interest: archaeology, psychology, and being a detective. Becoming a therapist was a natural evolution for me.

The other reason why I became a feminist therapist was again my own family history. Some of my cousins grew up before me in the 1930's and became what we now call "politically correct". I learned about racism and classism at an early age. At an anti-racism workshop in which I participated several years ago we were asked to recall the first time we each became aware of our own skin-color and that there were other skin-colors. My particular memory was of an older cousin playing "Strange Fruit" on the piano and explaining the lyrics to me. The song was written by Billie Holiday and was about lynching—still occurring in the 1930's in the South. My social consciousness was aroused early. I read our local (New York City) radical newspaper, *PM;* I went to demonstrations, went on marches, and took part in anti-war activities. Becoming a feminist was a natural step.

The last determining factor that led to my becoming a therapist was that I became, as a child, the family social worker. My parents frequently used me to resolve their conflicts. I find this to be a common experience in the histories of therapists I know. I learned to behave this way around friends, too: always the one who "understood," and was called on to mediate.

I dropped out of college very early to marry and had one child. I separated from my husband late in 1958, at a time when the women's movement and the social revolution of the 60's were being born. I returned to New York City from the suburbs and marriage, and found a group of new friends like myself. We were young, freshly divorced or single, working, going to school at night, and in therapy. My group of friends revolved around a training institute whose focus was interpersonal, and, by intent, anti-racist, anti-classist, and anti-traditional. They were forging a new lifestyle that attempted to break down old social customs including sexist behaviors. This group later became too insular and self-destructed but in the late 50's and 60's it was innovative, exciting and ground-breaking. Through my 30's and into my 40's my life consisted of work by day, school at night, and a few hours almost every evening with friends studying and talking endlessly about life and work and the changing times.

With my friends, many of whom would later be my colleagues, we spent hours dissecting the mores of what James Thurber called the "War Between Men and Women". Much of it was funny; much was deadly serious; most of it was new and thrilling. It still seems to me a wonderful time to be alive. I can remember explaining to others that I did not need to re-marry; that I could pay for my own dinner; that love, sex and romance were changing and that women had different choices, all issues that were to become the content of feminist therapy.

I was working my way through school and into a career. When I completed my bachelor's degree at 39, a friend asked me to join him in an administrative role at an Community Mental Health Center at a New York hospital, so that I could be in a position to earn the credentials to become a mental health professional. I had completed most of my course-work for a Master's degree. I spent the next several years in this program, acquiring the M.A., doing the course-work for a doctorate in clinical psychology, and gaining experience with a variety of client populations. This program existed in a healthy political environment. We participated in political demonstrations and marches for civil rights and against the Vietnam War. I think I went on every big march in New York and Washington in the 60's and 70's.

I am not certain when I first heard the word "feminist." I know that by the early 70's, it was part of my work. When I began private practice about 1970, women's changing roles were part of the content of my style as a therapist. My own interpersonal analysis was the core of my work as a therapist. It was an easy transition or merging of interpersonal and feminist. I was fortunate in that I did not need to burrow my way out of a personal traditional psychoanalysis nor ever go through any training that was sexist. All my early training was interpersonal with a heavy focus on doing non-traditional interventions.

During these early years of my education as a psychotherapist, I was not directly involved with the women who were forming the beginnings of feminist psychology. I was not aware of feminist psychology in academia nor was I aware of feminist therapists outside my circle of friends until about 1975. From then on I was networking and building new contacts. By the end of 1974, I had left my hospital job and was in private practice only. I had found the political environment more restrictive than was to my liking in the medicine-psychiatry setting.

During the 1970's, I began meeting feminists who became friends and colleagues over the years. Some were therapists, some not. I discovered the Association for Women in Psychology and joined the New York chapter. There I met and eventually worked with Barbara Sang, Leonore Tiefer, and Ethel Tobach, among many others. After attending the AWP conference in March, 1978, in Pittsburgh, I became more deeply involved. I was a member of the administrative board, the Implementation Collective, from 1983 to 1989. This group, more than any other, was a source of training and communion for me. Our conferences and meetings were always refresher courses in feminism. Another organization in which I have been involved is the Feminist Therapy Institute. I have been a member since 1986 and on the Steering Committee from 1988 to 1992. The experience of building and maintaining these organizations has been a vital part of my feminist identity and provided me with a setting in which I have felt at home in psychotherapy. I have presented several papers at AWP meetings and participated in writing and editing books with other members (Howard, 1986 (1); Lerman & Porter, 1990 (2); Chrisler & Howard, 1992 (3)).

My training as a feminist therapist took place largely at these conferences and training seminars, and by reading and practicing. In effect, we learned from each other, through our presentations and writing.

Another important part of the development of feminism was the consciousness-raising group. I remember meeting in the early 1960's; several women converging in one place trying to start talking about ourselves in relation to the world. Over the years, these meetings involved two or three women to many more. Some years later, the National Organization of Women developed an outline for groups of women to follow in order to facilitate talking and sharing.

This was an exciting time, during the 1960's and 1970's, women talking, writing, and meeting to share experiences and ideas. I recall the new "women's" bookstores at which we attended readings by feminist writers.

It has been a long, rewarding career for me—to be practicing feminist therapy. I've seen a new generation of feminists grow up in my practice. Young women of 30 now are quite different from the way I was at that age. They are more assertive, self-confident, and take many more things for granted that were denied to women 30 years ago. I am particularly thrilled to see young women entering into professions that were not open to me.

Although I identify myself as a feminist therapist, I have specialized in couples' therapy. From my earliest days as a therapist, I regarded relationships as two inter-twined sets of needs, not as something apart from the two individuals to be preserved at any cost. Whether it is short-term counseling or long-term therapy, I enjoy working with couples both gay and straight. I have found that feminist principles work with same-sex or opposite-sex partners. In addition to this special interest, another developed without my intending it. Over the years, my women clients often sent their partners, male friends, and brothers to me. I had not intended to become the feminist therapist who specializes in raising the feminist consciousness of males. I like men, however, and enjoy working with them. For almost all the years I have been in private practice, I have had 50% male clients. I always understood my role as a woman in our American culture. I find it fascinating to hear men talk about how they learned *their* beliefs and attitudes about women. As happiness is often perceived to be found in the other's backyard, power is often perceived to be found in the purview of the other sex.

There are some issues that feminist therapists often discuss about which I feel strongly. I support personal disclosure, with some limitations. I believe the therapist and client are peers. The difference is that one is an expert in interpersonal relations and in gender bias, and is helping the other to find growth and knowledge. I also believe that disclosing my experience that may parallel that of my client is a validation for her/him, reinforcing the conviction that we both belong to the same human race, and that s/he is not alone with it. Harry Stack Sullivan wrote that we are all "more simply human than otherwise." I believe that it is part of the therapist's job to reinforce that. The therapist should place the limits at the client's capacity to feel adequately comfortable with the therapist. This is a sensitive area. The differences between individuals can be subtle. Self-disclosing may not be something beginning therapists should do. Certainly the more private the area, ie: sex, the less it should be shared. Boundaries are another sensitive area. Feminist therapists often find themselves in overlapping social or professional circles with clients. I believe the bottom line is no exploitation of clients for any reason; no favors, not even trading of services. Therapy is a special situation. We are asking clients to trust us in special ways with very private feelings and information. There is no reason to clutter this special relationship with other needs and issues that might best be handled elsewhere. If a therapist takes chances on violating the trust of a client, the result may be the permanent withdrawal of the client from seeking the benefits of therapy from any other clinician.

I would like to address the differences in content in therapy between 20 years ago and now. In the early days of my practice, women were presenting hard-core issues of the powerful gender bias they encountered then. Women's presenting issues were mostly about interpersonal relations and efforts to change the ways they related to men. They also talked about work-place issues: sexual harassment, low pay, lack of respect. Currently, I find that women take for granted the changes so far attained. They think these problems still exist but find them more difficult to "name." The past 30 years have been a transitional time for women and men. I think it has been and is still difficult for the sexes to relate socially and in the work-place. The changes are still going on. Women are still struggling with their roles. They are still talking about being domestic slaves in the home and about being treated as children there and in the work-place. Women are still struggling to manage home, family and job simultaneously. Men are still quibbling about the ways and the amount they are willing to share domestic responsibilities. It is hard for both sexes and it is still in process. Working out these issues is much of what goes on in therapy for women and men.

I would like to say something about working with gay and lesbian clients in the 1990's. There is much more openness in our culture than there was 20 years ago but it is largely superficial acceptance by the larger community. I think there is as much disdain in much of the "hetero" community as ever, and that there exists merely a pretense of acceptance of the non-heterosexual lifestyle. The problem for gay people is still how to survive in a biased society, despite the increasing numbers of gay people.

I believe the same is true for people of color. Despite the apparent changes in recent years there is much need for help in therapy for gay people and people of color in the struggle against ever more subtle forms of bias. Feminist therapy is the best formulated of all therapies to help all clients.

Currently, in addition to a small practice in feminist therapy in San Francisco, to which I moved from New York in 1989, I am working in the field of social rehabilitation—where I began many years ago. As a clinical supervisor and an administrative person, I find feminist therapy as relevant to this setting as to private practice. Women in crisis are particularly disenfranchised. When I run a group or have an individual meeting with women who are in only brief contact with me, I find a profound response to the feminist issues I raise for them. Gender bias is well known to women in crisis. My current experience reinforces for me the substance and quality of feminist therapy. As I suggest above, it seems to me to address all variables such as sex, age, economic situation, and class, better than any other therapeutic orientation.

So I think, after having practiced it for more than 20 years, that feminist therapy is as important and viable as ever. It is going to take more than one generation for gender bias to disappear from our culture. Our clients today are still coping with conflicting messages learned from parents and community about women's roles. Change has occurred, but we still hear the same complaints. It is my belief that feminist therapy has barely begun to take the important place it will some day occupy in our society.

REFERENCES

1. Chrisler, J.C., & Howard, D. (Eds.) (1992). *New Directions in Feminist Psychology: Practice—Theory—Research.* New York, Springer.
2. Howard, D. (Ed.). (1986). *Dynamics of Feminist Therapy.* New York, Haworth Press.
3. Howard, D. (1990). *Competence and self-evaluation in psychotherapy.* In Lerman, H. & Porter, N. (Eds.) *Feminist Ethics in Psychotherapy.* New York, Springer.

III

THE EARLY
EXPERIENCES OF
FEMINIST THERAPISTS

6

Making Changes

JOAN HAMERMAN ROBBINS

> These places of making changes are dark because they are ancient and hidden; they have survived and grown strong through darkness. Within these deep places each one of us holds an incredible reserve of creativity and power, of unexamined and unrecorded emotion and feeling. The woman's place of power within each of us is neither white nor surface; it is dark, it is ancient and it is deep.
>
> Audre Lorde, *Sister Outsider.*

As a little girl I was fascinated by the many stories my grandmother told of her childhood in Minsk, Russia. Born to poor Jewish parents, her father died of tuberculosis when my grandmother was three years old. The only work her widowed mother could find was as a servant to a very wealthy family who would not permit her child to live on the premises. What happened to my grandmother because of these circumstances was told in one particular tale I never forgot.[1]

Grandma's mother figured out that the only way she could keep her child with her was to hide the child—in the closet of her room. There my grandmother remained. Hidden. Time passed. She never said, and I never asked, how long she was there. When I think about it now a shiver still runs through my body. Imagine a child hidden in a closet, food sneaked in to her, never being allowed to run around, play outside, or make noise. Her very survival is based on acting as if she does not exist.

In my childhood, I had an experience very similar to my grand-mother's. It was buried so deeply within me that I did not even real-ize it. I would not be able to reclaim this chunk of my past until I had several years of my own psychotherapy, which grounded me more firmly in my own identity and enabled me to accept myself. Then, in my late twenties, when I was pregnant with my first child, fragments of memories began to surface. The prospect of becoming a mother, with all its excitement and anxieties, aroused the memories of my most profound childhood experience.

Off and on over 25 years, bit by bit, with the help of three different psychotherapists—two women and a man—portions of this life-shaping ordeal have been retrieved. Through the relationship that developed with the therapist, I came to trust myself sufficiently to face the feelings I previously could not face alone.

Out of the experience of my own reluctance to acknowledge what had been so disabling to me and my resistance to knowing what I feared, I came to understand why the pace of psychotherapy is slow. In time I also appreciated how very fragile a person can feel as well as how cunning she can be about not revealing herself. No matter how many roadblocks and detours I erected to protect myself from find-ing out what I had been afraid to know, the therapist's skill and sensi-tivity enabled me to stay with what was happening. I am deeply grateful. None of this has been easy. For me, it has been very worth-while.

Years later while writing *Knowing Herself*, I recalled afresh the im-portance of my own therapy. My appreciation for that process fueled the desire to communicate to others how special and enabling thera-py can be.

THE EVENTS

The time was 1936, in the midst of "The Great Depression." My family was poor. My father was employed sporadically and spent his days looking for work. My mother had a part-time job. Suddenly, I became very ill with rheumatic fever. Bed rest was the only treatment; penicil-lin had not yet been discovered. I was four years old.

Each afternoon at one o'clock, my mother went off to her job and left me alone in the house, in my crib, for about two hours. Around three o'clock my 13 year old sister would return home from school.

Every day, for about three months, I spent two hours, alone, confined in that crib, waiting—waiting for my sister to come home.

Hired baby-sitters were rare in those days and there was no money for one, anyway. Nevertheless, it still does not make sense to me why a neighbor or a relative did not come and stay with me. What about my father? Or teen-age brothers? Why were none of them available to watch me while my mother was at her job?

The care of the child is women's responsibility. Men are excused. They go to work or look for work. In any case, whatever they are doing is more important than being involved with the nitty-gritty details of daily family life. Even though my mother was not handling this well she did not ask for help, and my father did not seem to notice what was going on. I never questioned my father's judgment while I was growing up. I respected and obeyed him. I'm sure I also respected and obeyed my two much older brothers. However, they did not respect me as an individual with distinct needs. They were distant —unavailable when I needed them the most. Now, that feels very sad.

I was fortunate to have an older sister who cared. She wore the nurturer's mantle in my family. She already had comprehended her role. Satisfaction and approval both were earned by paying attention to someone else's needs. She did not consider her own.

For my mother to have asked my father to stay with me would have established her as a person deserving of respect and commanding her share of authority in the family. Not only would she have been requesting legitimate help, but she deserved cooperation. She was the major breadwinner. However, such assertion was outside my mother's experience. It also would have been a blow to my father's pride and upset the family balance. That might have had consequences for my mother. Inadvertently, I paid a large price while my mother subordinated both her needs and mine to protect my father's dignity and a crumbling status-quo. I also speculate that my mother, unaccustomed to acknowledging her own needs and finding acceptance for them within the family, could not imagine that mine were being trampled over by her negligence.

As I began to recover from my illness, a doctor at a large city hospital who was supervising my recovery suggested to my mother that in the summertime she send me to a convalescent home for sick children at a nearby seaside resort. He told her, "It will be good for Joan." My mother did not question his judgment. She accepted it. One day that fateful summer, my mother took me out to The Home. She believed she was taking me there to recover. I felt I was being left to die.

Even now, after all the work I have done in therapy to remember this series of terrors, the middle part still remains buried. I have been able to put together the beginning and the end. I recollected being pushed away by my mother. I was clinging to her and screaming. I was terrified of being left. The only way she could get free of me was to push me away from her—into the hands of a matron who walked me down a long corridor. We entered a large room filled with cots. A cot and a metal locker for my clothes were assigned to me. I was handed a uniform and told to take off all my clothes and change into it. I would wear this uniform while at The Home. A second profound assault. First, I am separated from my mother. Then, from my clothes. I was thoroughly shaken.

I know I grieved and grieved and could not adjust to what was happening. I missed my family and the familiar surroundings of my own home. I thought I would never see them again. I was frozen in time. Numb. Nothing mattered. My way of coping with all these changes and the inner turbulence they created was to grow quiet, withdraw, and stop eating.

In one therapy hour, I vividly recalled these memories. It was suppertime and we children were all seated at long wooden tables. I glanced up from the table and noticed a side door, open to the street. Suddenly, I noticed my mother walking down the street—*away* from the building. Total confusion. How could I make sense of that? Why was she out there? Why was she going away? Doesn't she know I'm here? Why don't I call out! More terror. Would I ever see her again? Was she abandoning me forever?

Thinking about this now, I can not imagine how I ever got up from the table that night or went to sleep. The very next day my mother appeared and I was released. Years later, when I reviewed these memories with her, she said: "They wouldn't let me see you the day I came to make arrangements to take you home. They felt it would upset you."

THE HEALING

I grew up in a time and in a family that was oblivious to the nuances that color important life events. We did not pay much attention to our own or each other's disturbing emotions. We certainly did not discuss them. I know we did not talk over my absence or return. Most likely both my parents believed it was best put aside, now that it was over. It was expected that I would pick up my life as if nothing unusual had happened.

Soon afterward, I started school. When I tried to gain my parents' approval for my fledgling achievements they belittled me and my accomplishments; they dismissed me by changing the subject. I felt rejected and neglected by their lack of responsiveness. I was not rewarded for my curiosity and love of learning; my interests were ignored and I felt demeaned for being myself. Like many other girls, I was learning approval is secured by muzzling my initiative and subordinating my needs.

Both psychotherapy and writing have provided me with the means to heal these childhood wounds. Each time I have opened up this ancient misery, I have felt the horror of it. The pain was intense and I wanted to flee from it. Despite all that, I have been astounded that I have actually grown from reliving this nightmare. Each fresh excavation yielded both a new tender shard of myself that I had not know was there and released long-denied emotions. A flood of energy also accompanied each reclamation. Once expressed and accepted, these previously discounted experiences yielded new perspectives of myself. I became more expressive of the love and caring I feel for the people closest to me. I felt more complex and complete.

A particular time stands out in my mind. I was in therapy with a woman Jungian analyst who was very nurturing and empathic. She encouraged me to use art materials to feel my way back to the old pain. In one session, I finger-painted vertical lines and was quite astounded as I realized they resembled the slabs of a crib. I wept as the terror and isolation I had felt left alone in the house, in my crib, was re-awakened.

Following that release, creative energy burgeoned forth. I began to write. The article, "Breaking the taboos: further reflections on mothering," would be published in 1980 in the *Journal of Humanistic Psychology*. It is significant that my first writing was about motherhood, a role I had been putting much energy into for many years. Three books, popular at that time, revealed new perspectives on the cultural expectations of mothering: Adrienne Rich's *Of Woman Born*, Dorothy Dinnerstein's *The Mermaid and the Minotaur*, and Nancy Friday's *My Mother/Myself* provided the basis for my reflections.

While writing my article I asked my therapist if she would read it. She responded positively. I recall what a special moment that was. She was the first woman to support my creativity without hesitation. It made a great impression on me to finally receive what I had yearned for and previously been unable to obtain.

THE IMPACT OF THE WOMEN'S MOVEMENT

The Women's Movement was gaining momentum around the same time. An excitement and sense of expectation—change— characterized that time. The experience of women, which had been trivialized for so long, now became central as other women openly told their stories. I joined in that sharing and also led women's groups in my practice. I read avidly, becoming acquainted with ideas put forth by Phyllis Chesler, Nancy Chodorow, Shulamith Firestone, Kate Millet, Juliet Mitchell, Robin Morgan, and Gloria Steinem. The "Aha" was loud and clear. Many previous confusions now made sense. My personal and professional life were irrevocably altered.

Prior to the movement's impact, I had the major responsibility for running the household and paying attention to the needs of my husband, Bill, and my two children, Saul who was 12 at the time, and Rebecca, aged 11. Bill worked full-time. Although I worked part-time in my private practice of psychotherapy, like my mother before me, I felt the care of the family was mine alone to manage.

The insights generated by the Women's Movement provided me with a fresh perspective and validation for my feelings. I spoke up about the changes I would like to see in the way our family operated. Everyone became responsible for participating in household chores. It was not simple to make these changes; there were protests and discussions. My perseverance and commitment to the idea of equality and the goal of shared responsibility stayed firm. Gradually the family changed. In fact, they grew to enjoy their participation. We all learned to vacuum, cook, market, and do laundry. Everyone became a good cook and it was fun to watch what would appear on the dinner table.

My self-assertion created conflict between Bill and me. We were both unaccustomed to my being an equal in the relationship. Moreover, Bill felt threatened by my increasing activity in the Women's Movement. These were definitely rocky times. However, our deep caring for one another led us to fashion a way for handling differences and discomfort so that we each could grow from them. Our willingness to stick with the struggle enabled us to reinvent our relationship. Neither of us could have imagined the vast range of possibilities that opened for us both, individually and as a couple.

The feminist perspective burgeoning in the 1970s encouraged me to seek out other clinicians, especially women with whom I could share this excitement. In 1974 I joined the planning committee for the first San Francisco feminist-oriented conference on Women's Mental Health.

This was my first experience helping to organize a conference, creating ways for women from many different walks of life to work together. It was also my first opportunity to work more closely with lesbians. Some lesbians expressed hostility toward heterosexual women, especially if our partners helped support us financially. This was a sensitive, consciousness-raising experience. Sometimes there were hurt feelings and disappointment. I remember feeling sad about these gulfs between us.

The original enthusiasm which had us thinking we women were all alike didn't prepare me for dealing with conflict and differences. That was something I would learn over the years. These differences needed to be talked about. Heard. Once that was possible we could move forward to mutual respect. Two years later, I was pleased to be invited to present a clinical example of my work with women at a local training institution. I did not appreciate that in a tradition-oriented agency, my work could be perceived as quite radical. While generating enthusiasm from some people, my presentation also generated heated, negative responses from many in the audience, some of whom were women colleagues I had once worked with closely. I was quite overwhelmed by the negative reactions. It took some time before I could realize something useful might come out of this.

In the sisterhood of the 1970s I participated in the sharing that sometimes went on between some feminist therapists and their clients. I believed that discussing my own experience communicated the range and diversity of options available to women; it also demystified the therapist and the therapy process. We were two women working together, one of whom was in need of the services and skills the other had to offer. However, over the intervening years, I have now come to appreciate other, more complex reasons for generally not sharing my experience or opinion in the therapy hour. Women who come to therapy, like most women in this culture, have been repetitively conditioned to pay attention and focus sensitive awareness on other people. These skills make some women extraordinarily alert to the cues put forth by others. Not only has that been a consequence of female role conditioning, but it has become a survival skill as well. Once that talent springs into operation, many women lose sight of what they want or need for themselves. By not interjecting my experience, the focus remains with the client.

Another important influence was Jean Baker Miller's book, *Toward a New Psychology of Women*. I learned that she was organizing the annual Women's Institute at the Orthopsychiatry meeting in 1976, which I attended. Following that conference, I became actively involved in the Institute planning committee, getting acquainted with a wonderful group of women who were all concerned with developing and expanding a feminist perspective in psychotherapy.

My skill at clarifying this perspective sharpened as I had opportunities to participate in the yearly program. Ideas originating in these experiences laid the groundwork for papers I would write. They later appeared in *Women Changing Therapy: New Assessments, Values and Strategies in Feminist Therapy*, published in 1983. I co-edited this volume with Rachel Josefowitz Siegel whom I had met at the Women's Institute. We worked together on this book, creating a partnership that not only respected who we both are but each of the many women who contributed to this anthology. In keeping with our feminist principles, the essays in *Women Changing Therapy* reflect more than one style of exploring knowledge and communicating differences. The writings also reflect work by unpublished authors as well as more experienced writers and practitioners.

Through Rachel, in 1982, I became acquainted with other women who were starting the Feminist Therapy Institute, an organization to bring together experienced feminist clinicians and academicians devoted to sharing and expanding our knowledge about women. I am still active in this organization, which has offered me a nurturing environment in which to develop my ideas and extend my awareness into new realms. For the past few years, our organization has been committed to working on our internalized racism. We recognize that, as an organization of predominantly white women, each of us has some personal work to do before we can become a truly multi-ethnic,integrated feminist organization.

MORE CHANGES

As a result of this new awareness, I now spend part of one day a week at an adult education school where most of the students are women of color. These women, all mothers presently receiving public welfare, originally dropped out of high school. Now they are enrolled in this program to obtain their GED. I see several women for individual therapy and have led a women's therapy group at school. I have learned much as I became acquainted with the realities of these women's lives. Daily, most of them juggle complex responsibilities to get to and stay in school. As their involvement in the program grows, their determination to succeed heightens. I feel privileged to be part of this school.

The writing I contributed to *Women Changing Therapy* sparked my interest in writing my own book. This time I wanted to concentrate on women's issues in psychotherapy. By using the detailed knowledge that women share in the therapy room, I would demonstrate that the constrictions society places on women has had disabling consequences for them. Of course, that same knowledge illuminates the strengths and coping skills that most women acquire to survive in a culture that trivializes their uniqueness.

At times, as I wrote *Knowing Herself: Women Tell Their Stories In Psychotherapy* (published in 1990) these labors felt very overwhelming. I found myself confronting old terrors and anxieties; I lost and regained confidence innumerable times. I learned anew to trust the me who had been resoundingly stifled, first by the practices of my family, and later by the values and attitudes of the culture. Like many other women, I had never been valued for my distinct pursuits by my family of origin. Those early wounds had left a deep reservoir of self-doubt that had to be overcome.

In persevering I finally recognized that I was no longer a frightened, resourceless little girl who had been trained to devalue herself. I could trust myself even though I felt anxious as I grappled with the unknown. I could monitor my self-doubt when the going got tough without undermining myself. Although I received consistent support and caring from my husband, my daughter, my son, and a handful of close friends, these labors were mine alone to manage.

Another important outcome of writing *Knowing Herself* has been a boost to my self-confidence. I began to pay fresh attention to difficulties in my own life and to practice some of the suggestions I make in my book. In order to be heard and understood I have to speak out and stick with uncomfortable issues. Sometimes that includes making myself vulnerable; other times it means expressing anger or disappointment. Since the writing took several years, I was afforded ample opportunity for practicing. As I took more of myself into consideration and expressed what was important to me, I found understanding and acceptance.

Finally, my changed consciousness underscored for me the importance of political activism. While I had been active in political causes, especially the peace movement, my energy is now more directed to championing women's rights. Nowadays, women's right to choose is a dominant issue; however, that focus doesn't diminish other essential issues for women: equal pay and opportunity in the work-place, affordable and adequate child-care, and family-leave time that doesn't jeopardize one's job.

Keeping these issues central in daily life interactions is definitely an arduous task. Sometimes it can feel very lonely and unrewarding. Nevertheless, each time an individual woman takes the initiative and expresses what it is she wants for herself, or how she feels about what is happening to her, she confronts deeply embedded assumptions. By her actions she is changing both herself and the future for each of us.

NOTES

1. Portions of this essay first appeared in Joan Hamerman Robbins *Knowing Herself; Women Tell Their Stories in Psychotherapy.* New York,1990. Plenum. Reprinted by permission of the author.

7

My Story as a Feminist Therapist

ELIZABETH FRIAR WILLIAMS

I was born in 1931, in Buffalo, New York, and have been a feminist psychotherapist since 1969. From 1961 until 1967 I taught developmental psychology in New York City area colleges. When my second child was born in 1967, I wanted to work at home to be able to care for her, or at least supervise her early care, so, somewhat reluctantly, because I preferred academic psychology, I became a clinician. I grew to like clinical work much more than I ever thought I would and that is directly the result of the interesting clients I had at that time, the beginning of the feminist therapy movement, and the fascination of the feminist struggle in which I soon became engaged.

My psychotherapy training was with the New York Gestalt Institute but I learned feminist therapy with other female therapists in a peer group that we called the New York Association of Feminist Therapists. The others in the group at the time I joined, in 1971, were: Annette Hollander, Carol Gordon, Betsy Aigen, Barbara Suter, and Dale Bernstein.

A devastating personal experience in late 1968 focused my attention on feminism: my second husband, 7 years younger than I, and the father of our year-old daughter, admitted, after many denials, that he'd been having an affair with one of his sociology students, 23 years old, and that he intended to marry her. There was, he advised,

71

nothing I could do to affect this scenario: he would not go to couples' counseling; he prevented me from any input at all into the outcome of our marriage. He did exactly what he said he would do. The help-lessness I felt, as well as the intense rage, motivated me to seek pow-er, as always, through understanding. So, as always, when distressed, I read. The writing that made the most sense to me ex-plained my situation and feelings in feminist terms. I was particular-ly influenced by Phyllis Chesler's 1970 article in the journal *Radical Therapy*, which she later incorporated into three chapters of *Women and Madness (1972)*.

I had an unusual upbringing for a women of my generation be-cause my mother was an attorney, the only woman in her Stanford Law School class of 1926, and the only woman to take the bar exam that year in California. She might have been a positive role-model, but she had been a love-starved child, born in 1903. She lost her father to pneumonia when she was 2. Her mother was an abusive, para-noid, critical person who had a hard life as a young widow. She earned her living as a lace-dealer, traveling by boat to buy laces in Belgium several times a year. She took my mother with her, forcing her to entertain the passengers by showing off her skills as a child-prodigy at the piano even 'though my mother was chronically sea-sick. My mother never went to elementary school, but was tutored in Europe during her mother's visits there. Nonetheless, she gra-duated with honors from a girls' Catholic boarding school (my mother was Jewish) in the United States at only 15, and, from college, with a Phi Beta Kappa key, at 17.

My grandmother re-married when my mother was 14 and had a second daughter 17 years younger than my mother. As a parent, her-self, my mother's particular problems took the form of intense com-petition with me (as a stand-in for her sister, by whom she felt very threatened) hyper-vigilance, complete emotional unavailability, criticality, and an inability to empathize. She lied to get what she wanted from everyone, including her children, a characteristic she learned from her own psychopathic mother. I couldn't trust her and I feared her put-downs. Particularly painful to me were the lies she would whisper to my father about me, behind closed doors, saying that I was lazy, stupid, and disobedient. Because of her intelligence, assertiveness, and apparent self-confidence it was impossible for me, as a child, to contradict her.

I was saved from dire emotional problems because I had a loving, if formal, paternal grandmother in Buffalo and other accepting adults in our extended family and social group. My mother's young sister became a warm and valuable role-model for me after I moved to New York. She is only eleven years older than I and had an unusually successful career as an advertising executive for a woman of her generation. She was throughout her full-time career, the happily-married mother of four (now grown) children.

My two younger brothers, as boys, had more prestige with my parents than I, but they, too, suffered greatly from the family pathology so it's hard to see them as "favored" males. Indeed, growing up, I tried to give them the warmth my parents could not, and frequently intervened between them and my mother. This drove a still deeper wedge between my mother, who couldn't tolerate my interference with her role, and me.

My father was a mild-mannered patrician, raised as the last of three children of a well-to-do Dutch-Jewish, assimilated family that had as little to do with Jews as possible. He was also an attorney by vocation—a vocation at which he worked in an unassertive way—more as a legal scholar. His avocation was classical languages. At his behest we all took many years of Latin; I took Greek, French, Russian, and German as well. My father was fluent in German and French, and throughout his life read Latin and Greek literature—reading to us, as well, in these languages as well as in German. My mother, of course, was fluent in French, having grown up for the most part, in Belgium. My parents were both accomplished musicians; I've already described my mother's expertise on the piano, while my father played the violin. After dinner they played duets that were pleasing to hear.

All of this gentility masked considerable turmoil and pathology, needless to say, particularly my mother's viciousness and my father's utter lack of awareness of our psychological situations and deference to his hostile and frightening wife.

At 18, between my freshman and sophomore years at Vassar, I became pregnant by a man who wanted to marry me and rather than have an illegal abortion (which my mother encouraged in order to hide my early sexual activity) I married him and lived with him in Buffalo for a couple of years. While having the baby set me apart totally from the other adolescent girls in my social group, it was a healthy experience for me. My baby son was the person who made me feel most loved and integrated. This is hard to explain, but from that time on I felt like an adequate personality, competent enough to face whatever difficulties life had in store for me, which turned out to be plenty.

When my son was about two, I left that marriage and moved back to my parents' house with my son. I lived with them so that I could attend the local university as a day student. My parents were glad to pay the minimal tuition because they were terrified (as they frequently reminded me) that I would be their dependent for the rest of their lives. There were many painful scenes relevant to that fear in my early adulthood. One, particularly unforgettable and painful, took place at Yale the day of the graduation of one of my brothers. My young son, then 5, and my parents and I were walking on the campus—I had already moved to New York—when my father turned to me and viciously, without provocation, said, "Don't you ever come back to Buffalo to disgrace us or try to get anything from us. If you do I'll have you put in an insane asylum." Since my parents were both lawyers who knew many judges in Buffalo I thought that legal commitment was entirely possible. But I never would have gone home to them again, anyway, and was mystified at my father's suggestion that I might and stunned by his hostility. I was also disturbed at the emotional impotence his words implied. Was my father that frightened of me, and so unable to deal with the problems I apparently presented to him? I was only 24 years old, with virtually no power in the family (or anywhere else, heaven knows), while my parents were respected professionals. Nonetheless, apparently my existence posed a formidable threat to them.

The whole scene there, in New Haven, was one which was replicated in varying degrees in many families of girls of my own and earlier generations, as we know from the tragic stories told to us by feminist historians and biographers. The brothers were graduating from a prestigious school, the sexually active and outspoken "bad" daughter is a disgrace to the family and has to be hidden or lied about and is controlled by the threat—or, in more than a few families, the actuality, of commitment to a psychiatric facility.

The fear of being controlled by powerful forces and feeling impotent to influence them on my own behalf was surely a consistent theme in my early life and motivated me to seek power through educating myself and then educating others through teaching and writing. So it is natural that feminism (and Chesler's book, *Women and Madness*) would appeal to me and that I would enlist my skills on behalf of other women who may have also grown up feeling powerless against hostile and defaming authority figures and a destructive social climate.

I stayed away from Buffalo, of course, and also tried as hard as I could to support myself and my son in New York. His father was an actor with virtually no income and we received nothing from him at all. I sold hats in a department store and attended City College at night in a Master's program. In those days City was the only place where you could work on a graduate degree at night. Tuition was $25. per credit which my parents agreed to supply, as insurance against my "dependency." At the department store I worked my way up to the advertising department, which was fun until I got fired for doing my homework on the office typewriter. I was denied unemployment insurance because the store claimed they offered me my old job back selling hats, therefore weren't really firing me. I declined the offer.

In those days (the mid-50's) there were no single-mother support groups, no parents-without-partners, no day-care centers, or women's groups of any kind. As it is now, private therapy was exorbitant. There were no support services at all for women who were not in a family network or married. A young woman alone with a child was in a very precarious social, economic, and psychological situation. That was the situation in which I found myself at 26.

When I was fired I lost our tiny apartment and I had to send my adored little son, then six years old, back to Buffalo, to his father's sister's family to live for a year. For a few months I couldn't find a job and had to live in a succession of rented single rooms in other people's apartments and then, ultimately, with my crazy, abusive grandmother (who also lived in New York). I didn't want my child to be exposed to her and of course didn't want him to be with my parents, but his father's sister and her husband were kind people with young children. This was the most crucial decision in my life. I knew that if I didn't stay in New York and complete the psychological separation from my parents, I would be destroyed, and I knew my son's well-being, also, ultimately depended on my being an intact personality. So I did what was necessary, separating from him with all the terrible grief for both of us that that meant. As a result of remaining in New York on my own—and in graduate school—I grew up as a relatively healthy adult, individuated from my destructive parents. Eighteen months after my son went away, I again found a stable job and an apartment and could have him back with me. We managed well enough after that. Today he is a healthy and loving man, happily married for many years and a wonderful father to two girls. I think he has some residue of that experience, shown occasionally in a too-angry exchange with me and in a heightened sensitivity to separation that seems to me to echo his grief, too, when he was just a little boy, but that may be only my fantasy and my own residue of guilt.

The self-esteem I derived from that early and successful struggle to survive my parents' and particularly, my mother's virulent antagonism formed the core of what I believe is a basically optimistic and stable personality. Life certainly presented me with subsequent difficulties but that early crucible toughened me and gave me confidence in my inner resources. Because I fully experienced the grief of the separation from my son and the absolute painfulness of the circumstances in which I had to live for awhile, I have never been particularly sympathetic to magical solutions as "psychotherapy" or to religion. No matter how much I prayed for some kind of solace during those early years in New York, none arrived. It seemed to me I was doomed to feel everything.

I told myself that it was a virtue not to avoid the awful emotional reality, but to work through it and come out a wiser and more competent person. I believe that I did that and am a better therapist and person because of it. Obviously, today I am not very sympathetic towards therapies that I consider superficial, although I can understand that people need support wherever they find it. But to me support is not work and I believe with the psychoanalysts that "working through" painful feelings is essential to good therapy—even if it is feminist therapy, not psychoanalysis.

My last and most successful therapy, from 1969 to the mid-70's, was with Dan Rosenblatt, my Gestalt therapist, and, ultimately, supervisor. He is a gay man, as were many of the Gestalt colleagues from whom I learned a good deal about liberation from traditional social roles. Gestalt training in general taught me to challenge traditional therapy models, too, and certainly gave me permission to be my own model, which it turned out I had to be, as a feminist therapist.

Along with other female therapists I was beginning to read about the need for a "feminist" therapy. I didn't know where one could find training in that, or even where one could find other therapists who practiced such a therapy. But I decided that I would figure it out myself. Most of the early feminist therapists decided the same thing. I immediately called myself a "feminist therapist" and put a card on the bulletin board of the Women's Center in West 23rd St. proclaiming that I did feminist therapy. I don't know whether I had ever heard the term before and I would like to hear from others about when they first heard the term "feminist therapy." This was in 1969, the same year that the Association for Women in Psychology was founded. I charged anywhere from $4–$15 dollars a session. At some point soon thereafter I found other female therapists who were trying to create and practice a feminist therapy, as I have described above.

For me, the most stimulating aspect of our bi-weekly meetings was looking at how our own socialization as women affected our therapy work—our counter-transferences, as the analysts would say. We were a congenial group and stayed together, with other members coming in gradually, for a few years. In the early 70's the NOW Psychotherapy committee was formed and I joined that, as well. This group was very much larger and had enormous problems. There were about 30 women from the outset, growing larger all the time. Its leaders seemed to me to be remarkably authoritarian who imposed a rigid structure and many "rules" and inflexible require-ments for membership and referrals. One exchange I had with one of the leaders has stayed with me. I was told that I had to have night-time therapy hours since "Most of our clients have to work for a liv-ing." As I had a young child at home, aged 3, I did not at that time work at night. I retorted that I, too "worked for a living" and had been doing so since I was 19 or 20. The feeling I and some others had was exclusion. This was exactly the opposite feeling one got as a member of AWP, which I had also joined. The NOW Committee was very offensive to me and particularly distasteful since it reminded me so much of my authoritarian and critical mother. I lasted about 3 years, but never felt at home in it.

The NOW experience notwithstanding, I had a lot of faith in femi-nist therapy and thought it was "the answer". I felt everyone should know about it. I still feel that way. I gave a paper in 1973 at the Ameri-can Psychological Association's annual convention in Montreal in what must have been one of the first symposia devoted to feminist therapy. The interest in feminist therapy at the convention inspired me to think about writing a book for the general public showing how socialization as "girls" affected women's lives in often significantly negative ways. I, myself, was always so empowered by books that I thought others would be, too. At that time I was particularly driven to reach the general public rather than professional readers but I have changed my mind somewhat about that, particularly since there are many mental health professionals who are still not familiar with feminist therapy or who may not appreciate its value. I had completed all the work and exams for my Ph.D at NYU, and wanted them to take my book, which has since become a classic, as a dissertation. They refused, and I never did write a traditional dissertation because I thought that would have no social influence, at all, and more than anything I wanted to influence others.

Notes of a Feminist Therapist was published in hardcover in 1976 by Praeger and in paperback by Dell in 1977. It sold well and affected many women's lives. I know this because of the many touching letters I received from readers. It really brought feminist therapy to the awareness of many women who were not mental health professionals although as it happened, many readers were female therapists who still tell me when I run into them at meetings that the book meant something to them as, for awhile, the only one "out there" who helped define for them what they wanted to accomplish as feminist therapists.

Notes of a Feminist Therapist kept me in practice for many years. Well over half my practice for 10 years came to me through the book. These were unusually interesting clients who were trying to raise their consciousnesses about feminism and trying to change their relationships accordingly. Many of them had been at one time or were simultaneously in consciousness-raising groups. About 3/4 of my practice were women, mostly white, mostly straight, and the rest were men, most of them sent to therapy and to me by the women in their lives. Lesbians wanted to go to the many excellent lesbian feminist therapists and the same was true with women of color. One of the shortcomings of my book and not only of my book is that it had relatively little to say about lesbians and nothing at all about people of color. The reason for that is that it was based entirely on my own practice so that was self-perpetuating. Today both the Feminist Therapy Institute and the Association for Women in Psychology have committed themselves to making their organizations and consequently, the therapists in them, more receptive to women of color, more aware of their own biases, and more sophisticated about their issues.

My chief supports for practicing and writing about feminist therapy in those days were, of course, the women in my feminist therapy peer group but also the men in my Gestalt practicum: Jerry Croghan, Don Resnick, Marty Seif, and for the years he remained with us, our supervisor, Dan Rosenblatt.

Another important influence in my intellectual as well as personal life, since 1970, was and still is, my married lover, a distinguished social psychologist—a scholar, like my father, whose work concerns social justice. He was, and still is, unfailingly confident in me when I am not, and has the capacity to make me feel organized and coherent, as well as loved, especially when I am feeling neither. Our relationship has been characterized by a gratifying mutual emotional and physical dependency, but of course, we've never lived together. At first I was frustrated by his desire to remain married, but later came to value his decision and benefit from it, as he does.

At 55 years old, in 1986, I moved to San Francisco where both my mother and one brother lived. My mother, brought up in the Bay Area, settled here again after my father's death in Buffalo in 1975. In 1986 my daughter had been away at college for a year. An environmentalist and outdoorswoman she showed no interest in settling in the East after college. New York, much as it had given me in my early adulthood, became unliveable to me in the yuppie years of the 80's; too expensive and too ugly, dirty, and violent. Too inhumane, I thought, in which to grow older. So I rescued myself for (at least) the 2nd time in my life and moved to California. Here, I re-connected with AWP, joined the Feminist Therapy Institute and the local chapter of The American Society of Journalists and Authors. (I had been, for many years, an active member of the New York chapter.)

My children are, in spite of my divorces from their fathers, happy in their work and love-lives. My son, born in 1950, is a journalist with the Associated Press radio network in Washington, D.C. As noted, he has been married for many years and has two daughters. My daughter, 17 years younger than her half-brother, is a very gifted writer of fiction and non-fiction. She was married in 1992 to the young man whom she had been seeing since she first set foot in college, in 1985. She is exactly the age now as I was when I was struggling in New York, the sole support of myself and my little boy, to begin my difficult struggle toward emotional maturity and autonomy. The contrasts are stunning. Her life is much more promising than mine seemed to be in my mid-20's. This is not only because she had a far better mother than I did, but because she is the direct beneficiary of our movement. The movement gave her the Pill, gave her the opportunity to give and receive sexual love without guilt and fear, gave her a long childhood in which to rehearse various options, gave her entree to an Ivy League school previously closed to women and to some good writing jobs directly on graduation from college, whereas in my "day" if you were a "girl" you started a writing career by being a secretary or filing pictures. My daughter and I have a close relationship which is all the more poignant to me because as a young person I never had anything like that with my own mother, something I still think about with regret.

There are at least a couple of miracles in my life: my relationship with my lover has survived for 24 years (in contrast to my short-lived marriages) in spite of the natural frustrations inherent in it and the geographical distance now between us. Even more startling, perhaps, my mother and I were on very good terms by the time she died, in 1991, at 88. She lived long enough for us to resolve some of our problems so that my memories of her will not be only negative. She was very receptive to my moving to San Francisco and was helpful to me here. (Of course, she understood how important it was to have a daughter nearby as she approached her final years.) Her personality problems were such that she had no intimate friends and several of her longtime acquaintances had died or moved away. So great was her need that she was almost able to convince herself that she liked me. I miss her very much and am glad that, while I still didn't know her very well, I had more of a "real" mother in my late middle age than I had ever known. And it wasn't too late.

I've never really practiced much psychotherapy in California, which is all right with me, although I have done part-time counseling in a private school and also taught part-time in a graduate psychotherapy program, neither of which I do now.

I much prefer the free-lance writing I do—mostly on issues relating to women's mental health. The free-lance writer's style of working is entirely congenial with my personality. I get very excited by certain topics and plunge into them with great curiosity and energy. Sometimes I finish the project, other times I tire of it and want to go on to something else that has caught my interest. I consider myself an independent scholar in the old and best sense of the word—unaffiliated academically, thus free to inquire into and write about any topic that interests me and free to drop it when I lose interest.

I tend to be an easy-going person, not given to obsessive work routines or anything else—so I like to be able to play whenever I feel like it, which is often. Mostly I play by reading or walking around my beautiful San Francisco neighborhood, or I chat with friends and family on the phone and also by e-mail. I like to write little memoirs and personal essays for fun and send them around to friends and family, many of whom are writers. Since my daughter is also a writer and well-educated reader, as I am, we talk a lot about books and writers. This has come to be one of my most gratifying activities.

A good role-model is another therapist/writer, Eleanor Hamilton, who lives in Inverness, Ca. Eleanor is in her 80's. She moved from the East with a woman friend, leaving grown children behind, retiring, she thought, from a busy psychotherapy practice. She built their home with her own hands in a fairly isolated community on a gorgeous shore line. Soon after she settled in, she realized the community needed sex education and counseling, which she provided; at first on a part-time basis. Before she knew it she had founded The Inverness Psychotherapy Clinic and contributes a weekly sex column to the *Point Reyes Light*, a Pulitzer-prize-winning newspaper. Every few months she drives at night for an hour on a very twisty road to the meeting of our writers' association, and occasionally we gather as a group in her beautiful home to enjoy a barbeque and good shoptalk with this remarkable woman and her friend. Now that's a role-model!

8

How I Became a Feminist Therapist

IDA P. TRUSCOTT

I was born in 1915 and I began early-on to be a feminist, not knowing I held that label. At 9 years of age, Sunday School was a problem. I was directed to attend church as women and children were supposed to do. I was not given a choice, and I resented this duty, my first obligation as a female. (My father did not attend!)

I soon learned many other "women's tasks": setting the table, drying the dishes, getting out the good Haviland dishes and putting them away when we had company. My father, his brother and our male cousins never helped with these chores, even in their own homes.

There were some compensations and cherished moments: I learned to milk a cow and pack raspberries for market, jobs of responsibility; play and be with my gentle maternal grandfather; occasionally to be carried up the stairs by my strong, energetic father, whom I both loved and feared. He was a benevolent despot at home. I listened to all the grown-up "man-talk," and decided then and there to be like my father. He didn't have to do dishes; he could talk about what interested him. People loved him and respected him, asked his advice about medical problems. I determined to be like him, a medical doctor. Surely then people—and he—would respect me and listen to me, and I could be and do what I wanted. I would not have to be quiet when he napped, be silent at the table, always be a dishwasher.

My father raised my sister and me, growing up on a farm in Iowa, as boys to work in the raspberry patches and grape vineyards; but, as girls, we were "protected" from the hired men who mostly gathered in the dairy barns. I learned at an early age to "lead" the hired hands and their families as well as the fruit pickers who came for work during the Depression, in the thirties.

My father was of the "old school"; i.e., Victorian and autocratic. We lived in the big house built by my maternal grandfather, who had home-steaded on land near Council Bluffs, Iowa. My father's parents had come from Massachusetts and Virginia by packet-boat, also to homestead on a neighboring farm. My background is a meld of the old and the new. My father was descended from Francis and Sara Eaton of the Mayflower. My mother was first generation Scotch and Swiss.

The big, new house had high ceilings and tall windows, and creaked and groaned when the winds blew. When I was fifteen, the old house burned down. It was touch and go to keep the new house from catching fire while we waited for the fire engine to arrive from town. Hysteria was rampant. My father organized the men. I stopped the wailing wives and showed them how to help contain the blaze. I thought how needlessly helpless and noisy they were; but my words were calming. I realized I had a gift.

In high-school I found myself giving reassurance and advice to many of my friends. We talked at slumber parties or at school before or after classes. Most of them were girls who seemed to me not to be able to think for themselves, couldn't stay on one topic long, were giddy and noisy chatterboxes. Counseling seemed easy and natural. My goal to become a psychiatrist was born.

In college I was single-minded, studying pre-med and psychology. But, during the Depression, I worked as a secretary for tuition, room and board and that discouraged me. How could I, I wondered, a woman, expect to go to med. school? At that time, loans were not available for women. I was independent, working and studying. I called myself "emancipated," although it seemed something was lacking and I felt very much alone. But I stayed with my early decision to work with people—"even" women. The religion of my mother did not "take" on me, but her influence did. My grandfather represented the "good in men," mankind and religion. I would believe in a "social" good, doing whatever was needed to promote human welfare. It was not until later that I would say, "welfare of women". I had wanted medical school, even while knowing I would be in a "man s world" and it would be tough going.

I dated every weekend and had many beaux. I felt I could "play" if I wanted because it was my own money I was using for college expenses. I had worked for two years between high school and college at a credit bank. As a graduation present, my father had given me tuition to our local business school. The men I knew in the 30s were really boys looking for the same as I, affection, but hardly able to give recognition. When I fractured vertebrae in my neck and back in a car accident, I went home for a semester. I renewed my friendship with a very serious young man who was home from the Naval Academy, Harry Truscott. He later became my husband. His respect and adoration, I couldn't resist.

In a state of rebellious insight, I burst with a desire to "make it better" for other women who also needed to be self-supporting. Later, I took up the gauntlet for them and for those whose careers might be interrupted by raising a family, as mine was, or who were forced to take jobs with lesser pay when the plums were given to World War II returning veterans. That happened to me, too.

When I became a therapist in private practice in Cincinnati and later in Aspen, Colorado, I saw mostly women clients. I felt I had "come home." Their concerns were my concerns. Like my father, I had so-called strong male characteristics. I could be logical and firm but caring. It wasn't until still later that I owned these traits as feminine strengths. Specifics of my evolution as a feminist therapist were different from my journey into feminism. I was self-taught, practicing with an eye toward how I would want to be treated if I were a client. As a psychologist participating in staff conferences, my guiding tenet was to allow clients to speak for themselves. I determined as a therapist to be different from how the senior research psychologists at Harvard' s Psycho-Acoustic Laboratory treated me as a junior research psychologist when I worked there in the 40s. Staff meetings were closed to junior staff, but they were expected to conduct the experiments according to the pre-arranged plan of the senior staff.

I resigned from my first post-doctoral job as assistant-professor at Xavier University because of lack of confidence on the part of the department head, a man who did not understand my different style and vocabulary. In my lectures, I was beginning a new, informal approach and entertained extensive class discussion. This allowed for a less structured kind of learning, which proved to be especially appropriate for women at that time of revolution and rebellion—the 60s.

I have not experienced physical violence or abuse in my life and career—only male competition, "put-downs," criticism, "bad-mouthing" by colleagues and professors. I regretted having no women career models to follow. I admired not only my caring, bright and strictly volunteer mother, but also professional women who were like her. I was sometimes infatuated with Jane Addams of Hull House or my mother's younger friend, a single woman who was the Farm Bureau Home Demonstration Agent for our county.

My search for understanding myself as a woman has been an intellectual challenge in which I related to the universe of women while wanting and seeking respect in choices primarily open to men. My search has continued. For me, the conflict persists: identification with the male world but trained as a caretaker. The conflict of being born a woman and raised with aspirations to be a man continues as I job hunt now and face age discrimination against women.

IV

BEING OUR OWN MODELS AND INVENTING THE THERAPY OUR CLIENTS NEED

9

Feminist Therapy

LEE JOHNSON-KAUFMANN

I was born in 1942 and grew up in Southern California. I had many advantages as an only child of a loving family. My father adored me, my mother adored me and I was given the message very early in life that I could do anything I wanted to do. The downside of this was that it was difficult for me to see the sexism in our society until much later in my life. But the upside dramatically outweighed the disadvantages. My mother worked throughout my childhood and I knew her to be a strong woman. My father was loving and affectionate which gave me a positive feeling toward men as well. In 1964, I began working as a public health nurse in the County of Los Angeles and worked in a black ghetto. My political views were never the same after that. I became a radical leftist and rapidly evolved into a feminist.

While in nursing school at UCLA in the early 60's, I had the great pleasure of meeting some exciting and powerful woman professors. I was exposed to innovative and creative psychiatry and was immediately intellectually stimulated. I knew by the time I was 20 that psychiatry or psychology was the direction I wanted to go, although I didn't know how I was going to get there. I was stimulated by the knowledge of my own inner self as well as perceiving, for the first time, multiple layers of human behavior. I guess you could say it's been complete and utter fascination with the human creature, which led me to psychology and has kept me there for 30 years.

I have an incredibly powerful, sensitive and loving life partner. We are truly equals. Because he is an author and works predominantly at home, our son has grown up in a loving and most interestingly, different life. I often work in the evenings and spend time with my son on the weekends. The result is that father and son have an extremely close relationship.

My clients know a bit about my life. This varies with age and sex of client. Some of my older female clients seem to enjoy "mothering" me. I must admit I get a certain amount of satisfaction from that process as long as it doesn't interfere with the therapeutic process. I keep boundaries very clear, something that I did not do well when I was in my 20's. I have frequently used relationship issues between my husband and myself as examples for couples and sometimes individuals. With disclaimers for individual differences, I try to interject humor and self-reflection into the examples I share (an interesting story).

My female clients, in toto, have influenced and sustained my feminism and commitment to feminist therapy, as it were. The battered women, the women locked in by poverty and lack of education, the depressed and anxious women who are unhappy with their lives but can't change or won't change, all the pain these women share underscore the need for more and more equality.

My professional role models include Gloria Steinem, Helen Gurley Brown and Joyce Brothers. Although the therapist whom I saw while in graduate school was a feminist, I didn't bond with her enough to be able to model myself after her. The most influential mentors for me in graduate school were men. However, a very important role model for me was my own mother. She worked throughout my childhood and always appeared to be confident and her own woman. In retrospect I realize this was not always true but as a little girl that is what I saw. My mom and dad had very egalitarian roles in their relationship and I grew up to expect that in my own life.

Although I have not joined any feminist therapist groups, I have, off and on, been a member of the Association for Women in Psychology. Beyond paying dues, I have not contributed. My doctoral dissertation in 1977 was very feminist-oriented: "Looking At Sex -Role Stereotyping in a Total Health System", i.e., public mental health system in a county in California. It was an extraordinary opportunity to read all the feminist literature I had been wanting to read for a number of years. Although I did not advocate feminist therapy, per se, in my dissertation, it was clear that sex-role stereotyping was an important factor in the mental health system and my recommendations were to include gender issues in the programming for this particular mental health system.

When I was a young, naive public health nurse, I went to see a psychiatrist because I was concerned about my sexual arousal and ability to be orgasmic. He promptly proceeded to blame my problems on my "mothering" tendencies having something to do with the fact that I was a nurse. As a budding feminist, as well as a psychotherapist, I knew what he was telling me did not ring true and I chose not to return to that psychiatrist.

I have not received any formal training as a feminist therapist. I have believed throughout most of graduate school education that my professors, both male and female, treated me with respect and interest. This may have been because I was 30 when I returned to graduate school. Perhaps my confidence as well as my age contributed to the respect I commanded. While in graduate school, my two most influential mentors were men. One was a traditionalist, i.e., sexist but truly believed I was very intelligent and treated me likewise. The other was a true feminist and enjoyed a very egalitarian relationship with his professor-psychologist wife. I had no negative experiences throughout my five years of graduate school or the year of post-doctoral work.

My early clinical days were in public mental health. Most recently, for the past 12 years, I have been in private practice. Although the symptoms are not terribly different, the complaints around those symptoms have shifted somewhat. The increased awareness of substance abuse as an important factor in one's childhood has been very widespread in our society. This has led to a growing awareness among women who seek treatment and their desire to work on childhood issues. However, I must admit, that I am still completely amazed by the number of educated women who have little or no awareness of the pervasive nature of sexism in the American society. Many of these ignorant women are under 40.

I do have some concerns about feminist theory and practice as I have been exposed to it. I must preface with the disclaimer that I have not kept up with the latest research nor am I deeply involved in feminist therapy organizations. It's very important to me to "walk my talk" (do according to what I say I believe.) I feel that I practice feminist therapy every-day with every client population. I believe my life is a testimony to feminism. I am not convinced that feminist theory can stand on its own, exclusive of the position of sexist theory or male

theory. I do believe very strongly that feminism and feminist therapy
have made us, as a society, more aware of the inequalities present. I
also perceive that we are just now beginning to recognize that the differences between the sexes are very real but do not connote inferiority or superiority. The challenge of prejudice and sexism will
continue. But we feminists knew that from the beginning it would
take three generations to change. We have just begun.

My work as a therapist over the past 25 years has changed dramatically. From beginning deep in psychoanalytic theory and therapy,
moving through the touchy-feely evolution and revolution of the
60's and 70's, I was introduced to behavioral and cognitive psychology during my graduate program. Both behaviorism and cognitive
psychology have profoundly affected how I see people, the way
their mind works, and the appropriate interventions. My background in nursing (B.S. in nursing from UCLA) gave me, from the
beginning, a greater appreciation for the biology of the human. Ten
years ago I added hypnosis to my repertoire and expanded my interest in deep psychological work. The evolution of my therapy includes more direct suggestions about what can be done in short term
work and individualistic treatment planning. I have no set way that I
deal with a client. I tailor each treatment plan to the particular individual based on my evaluation, his/her motivation, and the presenting problem. Counter-transference issues (the feelings and attitudes
of the therapist toward the client) as a feminist come up primarily in
my expectations of women. I monitor those carefully and adjust according to what information I receive. With age and mellowing, my
expectations lack the fervor of my earlier days. I think in general
that's a positive direction.

It is clear to me that the role of the feminist therapist is that of being
a change agent. I chose over 20 years ago to declare myself a change
agent. I take responsibility for that position. I believe it to be my responsibility as a woman in the 1990s to educate and strengthen both
men and women as we move toward positions of greater equality.
For each man or woman that I help change, there will be a ripple effect among family members and perhaps in the work place.

Perhaps the most dramatic change in problems being presented
to therapists these days is that of the introduction of childhood incest and sexual abuse as therapy material. When I first began as a
therapist 25 years ago, it was not a subject that was discussed. We
had all read Freud and essentially believed in the rich fantasy life of
the woman as she plays out the "Electra" complex (erotic feelings,

usually unconscious, towards her father.). Now, the profession must deal with post-traumatic stress syndrome 25 and 30 years later, the result of incest that was only too real. I don't believe that feminist therapy differs from any "good" therapy. All therapists, male or female, who fail to alert their clients to sociological and cultural influences on personality and perception are negligent and doing a poor job.

I am currently writing a play-book on sexual therapy for therapists and couples. I plan to continue seeing clients for at least ten more years. My retirement will probably include more writing and seeing fewer clients. Because my husband is a writer we could both be mobile if I were also able to make a living at writing.

Feminism is a state of mind. Psychology is a wonderful profession within which to express that state of mind. Feminism is not only humanism but an attempt to look at the greater system in which people live. Any system or theory that blames without solutions will not move forward. I am concerned that we, as a whole, both male and female, will lose sight of cultural factors as they relate to our growing up, our personality development, both "normal" and psychopathological.

We must not lose sight of the intimate interactive effect—beginning before conception—of the environmental factors and biology. It appears to me that we are still restructuring our picture of the way things work both in the family and in society. An exciting challenge of being a psychologist is the volume of information we want and need to know. It is important that we do not get stuck in the immediate present. Feminist therapy is good therapy and must continue to evolve. Bringing up issues of blatant sexism and how research done on men has been incorrectly generalized to women have been very important contributions of the feminist movement in psychology. Perhaps it is time to consider greater and greater integration of all therapies.

Feminism has given me great pride in my person, my femaleness. I respect and cherish those of my qualities that are culturally defined as "feminine". I spent a lot of years in my young life trying to be "masculine" because, like a lot of women, I thought that was how you had to be, to be "successful." But I see now that that was wrong. All kinds of people can be successful from "feminine" to "macho." I rejoice in my femininity.

10

Feminist and Multi-Cultural Therapy

MARIA FADLI

I became a feminist by choice. I identified with the need for females to be in more equal balance with males. I felt an unbalance and inequality of things at an early age. At home, I was the youngest and the only girl of four children, having three older brothers, and elderly parents. I was treated different, having less freedom of expression, of choice, of actions, and significantly less power. I believed GOD created us (females, males) equally & to complement each other. Yet, the differences, favoritism, preferences, competitions, separation, privileges, sexism, and discriminations, were all present at home, church, school, cultural, social, economic, and political teachings. I resented this mode of thinking. I decided not to let it happen to me.

In my later days, I lived the everyday existence of the "lesser" sex. I experience the disparities of our indoctrinations, and upbringing, and rebelled to be treated less fairly, for no natural reason. I now want to be sure, my only daughter, whom is nine years old, is not shortchanged in life. I understand it is very important to be treated equally from the start. I remembered I was under the impression something was "less" with me being female, when my family used to refer to me as "chancleta" (old, broken shoes, relegate to be used at home only). So, my father will say, " I have three sons and one "chancleta". Moreover, people were very happy when they gave birth to boys and celebrated the occasion with gifts; most often, cigars were given to visitors, in contrast, the birth of a girl, was not seen as a happy occasion, neither celebrated as much, and if so, gifts were not customary. Men who fathered "chancletas" were subject to mean jokes and laughter, and the couple always hope that the next time it would be a boy. If gifts were exchanged, old, used-up things were given. This behaviour affected my sub-conciousness to feel that being a female was less than being a boy or at extreme case, even bad. I decided to make things fairer and to take things in my own hands to bring about changes in me and others.

I became a therapist by my own needs to be of service to the needy, and to provide answers to my questions, understanding to my confusions, and help myself at the same time I helped others to help themselves. I was aware of the sufferings of others and sensitive to the need of healing ourselves. I have also been aware of the need for support in the absence of family support. I believed in "extended" family support. I interpret that a therapist is an extended family member. I respect this relationship.

In intimate relationships I fit the lover, wife, mother, in me to a holistic experience. I welcome these relationships in my life as pieces to a whole. My clients knew about my life a whole lot at the beginning of my experiences as a therapist and when I was in much need myself. I overly identified, and symphathized. As I grew older, wiser, and more experience, I began to keep a larger space between my personal life and that of my clients in order to be fairer to them.

There was one client in particular who influenced and moved me. This was a woman much older that I was then, and who was from a different culture than I. She was more aware of feminist issues and shared her insights freely both in individual and group therapy. She explained that she was not able to respond to outpatient drug free treatment, because the programs were modeled for men, and did not contributed to wo"men's" enhancement, development, nor "empower"ment; therefore, they were not viable for treating wo"men." She also expressed that the terminology used was intended for "men", and that so many words with "man" or "men" as a part of it, were the most powerful and most used words in the English language. She listed words like **"human, mankind, woman, women, manpower, treatment, abatement, abdomen, amen, female,** etc. as examples, and she emphasized that as long as these and other words were used in the empowerment of non-males we were sabotaging our own efforts. I took note and assimilated the awareness to avoid using such words and to find alternatives to them.

My models were in chronological order (from childhood to now): Maria Felix, Julia de Buryos, Lolita Lebron, Eva Peron, Carmen Livigne (an "adopted mother" now 80 years old) Don Pedro Albisus Campos, Malcom X, MS magazine, and Madonna .

I further realized that therapy can be a mono-cultural experience and therefore ineffective for a great majority. Moreover, the word HE is most commonly used even when the sex is not defined, and to change to "she or he" when talking about both sexes has received with much resistance not only from men, but also from wo"men". I found it bad that the female gender is not given importance or usage and that professionals tend to use the male gender term, more often than not, as an example,. It has been a continuous occupation for me to learn female gender terms. I knew very well that in Spanish language for instance we use male and female words, ie: Doctor (male) Doctora (female) maestra, maestro, but even so there were words that did not have the female equivalent or when it existed, did not mean the same. For example, "musico" means male musician, but "musica" is not used for a female musician and it means "music". There is not a female-gender term for a female musician, she is called "musico" too. In English, I knew the difference from an actor, actress, waiter, waitress, but there are many terms for which I am still trying to find the female gender equivalent. I had a had experience with my business cards printer. I wanted my business cards to be both in English and Spanish. I provided the work translated and finished ready to print. When I picked up my business cards (five thousand) I found that he had correctly written "consultant" as my occupation as I had ordered, however, the translation for English I had provided was "Consultora," and he had written, "Consultor,," the male gender. I requested the business cards to be printed again with the right word. He insisted that it meant the same. I insisted that it did not mean the same to me and I did not wanted to be called "Consultor," and moreover, I had ordered him in writing to print "Consultora" in my Spanish written cards and he had chosen to change it. He claimed that he was a Master in Education and he had used the **right** term, and I was wrong in using "consultora', which did not exist.

Needlessly to say, I had to take the printer to court. It was not easy but I finally won the judgement and the business cards were corrected.

I have never received classroom training as a feminist therapist. I have life experiences. My most positive training experiences have been to meet both wo"men", and men who shared my uneasiness, anxieties or restlessness and worked together to improve the conditions, and learn from each other. My most negative training experience is the difficulty in finding up-to-date training materials.

I have doubts about the theory and practice of feminist therapy. In theory, I am one who believes in and advocates the same social, economic, and political rights for women and men. "Feminist therapy" however implies that feminism is a disease or disorder that needs treatment.

It implies that wo"men" are in more need of feminist therapy than men. It is like having "La Raza" studies only for Spanish or Latinos, as if they didn't know or were the only ones needing to learn. Or having Gay or Lesbian Studies only to Gays or Lesbians, as if they didn't know the issues. The practice of feminist therapy only to females is counter-productive.

I do not agree with the practice of self-disclosure to clients. I believe that if one is in need of self-disclosure, she should have her own therapist. Clients come to us for help. It is their time. They wish to be heard. Seventy-five percent listening, fifteen percent thinking, ten percent or less talking, should be our practice. What makes sense to us in this very moment may change tomorrow. Clients should be free to make their own decisions without being influenced by our own behavior or thinking. We are all different beings from different backgrounds. What are the purposes, results or benefits from self-disclosure? Approval, acceptance, role models, example, sympathy from the clients? Not necessarily so. It is too risky, an unnecessary step. I believe our behavior in sessions, our accurate feedbacks will speak for itself.

I see as the most important issues in feminist therapy today to be the lack of movement. The most frequent problems being presented by women are the separations of issues and dealing with the part and not the whole. I often hear also about the reluctance of men to undertake therapy. Women are more willing and ready to seek help and to recognize that help is needed than men. Men perceive therapy as "unmanly" and are not open to sharing their feelings, problems, confusions with a person outside the relationship. We must address the similarities and the differences of the sexes. We must work together to deal with the issues and mix up the sexes of clients and therapist, both in individual and group therapy. We are failing to bridge the gaps. We are conditioned to keep a separation between the sexes from childhood. We are never taught to work together to achieve goals. We see each other as strangers, yet we are expected to be able to deal with each other, work, love and survive together and get along. How can we? We must begin to close the gap and to heal each other together.

I am a multiculturally sensitive person, forty-one years of age, a lover of nature, happily married, with three children (two adult males, one female child) and a female dog. I have a B.S. in Human Services from Boricua College in New York, New York, and twenty years of experience as a Drug Therapist for Reality House East (N.Y., N.Y.), an adult outpatient drug-free and methadone treatment program for both females and men from multicultural populations. I was personally involved in making changes that would include therapy that took into account womyn's and children's needs. This is a program originally designed for men, by men, in which womyn had no chance of success.

Feminist therapy is a promise for the future. It is a pledge I have made and a project for life. There is great need to come together to heal each other. I believe feminist therapy can help us bridge the gap between the sexes and help us to better understand ourselves. With emphasis in Female, Femininity, Feminism, and Womynism, we can begin to put together the pieces.

We have to create our past as people, our herstory. We have to unearth our heritage from the hole where some men have buried it. Like archeologists, digging and sifting, exploring and guessing, we are finding and fitting together the fragments of a proud herstory. Yet we have only pieces and can only begin to imagine where they will lead and what we will someday know of our past. I can't imagine more because my imagination is still crippled from the scurvy diet of history I was fed in my classrooms.

If there is righteousness in the heart, there will be beauty in the character, Is there is beauty in the character, there will he harmony in the home. If there is harmony in the home, there will be order in the nation. When there is order in the nation there will be peace in the world. Womyn to Womyn, Hand in hand: The herstory of feminist therapy is a step in the right direction. A promise to the future. Peace to ourselves and for all. I will end my contribution with the following poem, dedicated to us all:

For every womyn who is tired of acting weak when she is strong,
*   there is a man who is tired of appearing strong when he feels*
*   vulnerable,*
For every womyn who is tired of acting dumb,
*   there is a man who is burdened with the constant expectations*
*   of "knowing it all,"*
For every womyn who is tired of being called an "emotional female,"
*   there is a man who is denied the right to be weak and gentle.*
For every womyn who is tired of being a sex object,
*   there is a man who must worry about his potency.*
For every womyn who is denied meaningful employment, with equal pay,
*   there is a man who must bear full financial responsibility for*
*   another human being.*
For every womyn who was not taught the intricacies of an automobile,
*   there is a man who was not taught the satisfactions of cooking.*
For every womyn who takes a step toward her own liberation,
*   there is a man who finds the way to freedom has been made*
*   a little easier.*

11

A View from the Prairie

ANN McCLENAHAN

"What is a feminist therapist doing in South Dakota?" This question is one I encounter often, usually asked by a woman whose employer has transferred her here. She has come to my office because of difficulty adjusting to the traditional, patriarchal, chauvinistic culture she has found.

"I grew up in this state," I respond, "and have responsibilities to aging parents who live nearby." In addition, I feel I am needed by my clients to offer a different point of view about the causes and treatment of women's emotional problems. The medical model of mental illness is in full force in rural America. Daily, I hear stories from women who have been victimized by this out-of-date and narrowly rigid philosophy. Some of these stories I will share with you later in this chapter.

First, though, a little input about my background. How did a conservative Republican from a middle-class family end up promoting feminist ideas? I certainly didn't start out that way. I feel I have led two lives: a traditional lifestyle for the first 35 years, and a non-traditional lifestyle for the next 25.

I grew up as an only child, probably spoiled by my parents and grandparents (I was an only grandchild, too.) School was always fun and easy for me. I skipped the third grade because after 2 months of it I was bored. I graduated from high school, having just turned 17, tied for third place in scholarship.

Following a year at a girls' college (with *women faculty*—unheard of in the 1950s), I transferred to the state university, graduating with a degree in psychology. There were no jobs for B.A. psych majors, but I had minored in elementary education and so was able to teach kindergarten for the next seven years. This was a job I loved and which I thought would be a good preparation for motherhood.

I married a law student who, eventually, established his own office. I then quit teaching and became a legal secretary to "help out" with his career. My intention was to have a family (I planned on two to four children), but there were infertility problems, not resolvable at that time. This was depressing to me, as was the realization that, while I loved my husband, I really didn't like him much. Our values were quite different and he was very self-involved. He had little to offer me emotionally. Still, the thought of divorce was anathema to me, so I remained married but withdrew from him, with predictable results. He became involved with another woman, a client , and wanted a divorce.

I found myself, at age 35, alone, unemployed, scared, and confused about the future. I had been away from teaching for seven years; I certainly couldn't make a good living as a legal secretary. My decision was to return to college to acquire a master's degree in counseling. Following graduation, I worked as a school counselor and psychometrist in a rural school system, grateful to be employed. Motivated both by a desire to learn more about the counseling field, and by a wish to earn a higher income (sensing that I would be self-supporting for many years to come), I returned to college to acquire a doctorate.

Having been brought up to believe in a just universe, I was shocked to discover, in my doctoral training, injustices against women patients acted out in mental health settings. Even the language of the diagnostic labels seemed like "put-downs" to me. My women clients were forever being categorized as objects: "schizophrenic", "manic-depressive", "borderline", etc. It seemed to me that these women were not only scared and insecure, but, in addition, the system designed to help them denied them their perceptions. For example, if they claimed to be victims of domestic violence, they could be, and often were, sent off to mental hospitals. Something wasn't right here.

When I inquired about safe shelters for victims of physical abuse, I was told that this wasn't one of the mental health center's concerns. But what was I supposed to do about the woman who called me in desperation and fear, wanting to know how to handle a husband who was threatening to kill her and her baby? Was I supposed to tell her that we didn't have any help for her? Or, as the local minister advised, tell her to "pray a little harder, and her husband would shape up"?

The trivialization of women's legitimate concerns deeply affected me. Little-by-little, I started to wonder why this had happened and what I could do about it. And so, my journey toward becoming a feminist therapist had begun. Every year, I progress a few miles further down the road of knowledge and personal understanding about women's issues.

The following composite stories, which have been altered and fictionalized in the interests of confidentiality, are from rural mental health consumers, and reflect their real-life concerns.

THERAPIST RAPE: THE ULTIMATE BETRAYAL

"He told me I could trust him—that he wanted to help me feel good about myself again."

Carol was a newly separated, not yet divorced, young wife and mother whose self-concept and emotional health were fragile from the stress of her long-troubled marriage to Donald, an accountant. She had grown up in a small town where she learned to trust the adults she came in contact with—her parents, her teacher, her minister, and her doctor. It was natural for her to also trust her therapist, a man to whom she turned for help when discouraged by her marriage.

But her trust, it this case, was misplaced. Her therapist, a man with impeccable professional credentials, seduced her into a sexual relationship that lasted five years before she could break it off. Meanwhile her marriage broke up, and her emotional health deteriorated to the point where she took an overdose of sleeping pills in an effort to end her life. By the time she got to my office (an act of will-power she didn't know she had), this former high school cheerleader, respected wife, and mother of three children, was obese, had thin, unhealthy hair, sallow skin, and a defeated attitude.

She blamed herself. Her former attractiveness had been labeled "seductive" by the therapist. She "knew" it must be true; how could such a knowledgeable man be wrong? He was so much more intelligent than she was (she had been an honor student), and he was so well-respected in her community. His wife and children were such nice people. Clearly, she was the one to blame for what had happened. But a little nagging voice (barely perceptible) kept telling her she had been "had."

Little did she know when she showed up in my office that she was not the first victim of this therapist to show up at my door. Even though his "problems" were obvious to me, I still was surprised and horrified at each one's story.

I am happy to report that after several years of therapy with a counselor who understood how the unequal power relationship of counselor and client contributes to client victimization, Carol happily remarried and is living a generally satisfying life. None of his victims pressed charges and the therapist, of course, goes on his merry way, adding a few new notches to his belt of "hits."

THE SHOCKING TRUTH:
THE CASE OF THE OVERDONE TREATMENT

Her grown daughter talked to me first, wondering why 50-year-old Joan had been having such difficulty remembering anything of the past 10 years. Actually, it all started when Joan entered a mental hospital for treatment necessitated by a severe reaction to the breakup of her long-standing marriage. Joan had been depressed and drinking a little too much; symptoms that prompted her doctor to recommend inpatient treatment.

So far, so good. Patients do sometimes need to be hospitalized for depression. In fact, they do sometimes (infrequently) need shock treatment for intractable, suicidal depression. What nobody could foresee was a goof-up in record-keeping which resulted in twice as many shock treatments as had been ordered by the doctor, who was gone on vacation! The mistake wasn't discovered for 10 days. By this time, Joan's brain had been "fried" too many times.

Today this woman, who has been unable to function independently since that time, cannot remember what day it is without referring to her ink–stained wrist (where she has copied it from the calendar). She cannot carry on any but the briefest conversations, forgetting what the topic is, and so has driven away her friends. Her daughter is afraid she will forget to turn off the oven, or put out her cigarettes but hates to put her into a nursing home yet.

So they continue, one day at a time, her daughter stopping in daily at her mother's apartment to check on her safety. Her mother is in her usual semi-haze of TV watching or re-dusting the furniture for the fifth time that day.

THE GOOD LITTLE GIRL

Debbie had been brought up to be a "good little girl"—the apple of her father's eye. Her father, an industrious Dakota farmer, saw to it that his only daughter got a good education, sending her off to a private college to learn nursing.

He was pleased when she married "well"—a bright medical student, Dan. Debbie, however, was finding out that not all men were like her father. While she had been rewarded with affection and praise for hard work as a little girl, as an adult woman working two jobs to support her medical student husband, she seemed to receive as her rewards only emotional neglect and verbal abuse. She justified Dan's behavior as the inevitable result of his high-pressured training program and tried to be patient.

Her husband eventually became a physician and the couple had 3 sons. As financial pressures lessened, life became more comfortable. Debbie settled into a routine of nursing, parenting her children, and being a wife. Dan was seldom home, and never spent time with his sons. But Debbie did not complain. After all, he was trying to build up his medical practice and be a good provider for the family, she told herself.

Imagine Debbie's surprise when she came home from school one day to find a note from Dan: "I have moved my things to an apartment and will be filing for divorce. There is nothing to discuss, so don't bother trying to talk me out of it." He left her his new address and phone number, and signed his name.

It turned out that some of the long hours Dan had been putting in were spent with his 23-year-old secretary/nurse in a personal, rather than a professional relationship. Soon Dan and Debbie were divorced, and he married the young woman.

Although it was difficult, Debbie finally "adjusted" to the divorce. She and her three boys got on with their life. Things again settled down to a routine of teaching and parenting her children.

She had not counted on Dan's need for power and control. To make a long story short, there were eight years of in-and-out-of court motions, depositions, orders, complaints, and assorted legal maneuvers whereby Dan tried to prove Debbie an unfit mother and obtain full custody of his sons. (This was a man who had no time for these boys when he was married to their mother).

After spending $100,000 of her own and her father's money to fight the never-ending court battles, Debbie ultimately lost custody of her children. It was a clear victory for power, money, and bullying behavior.

Dan did not win this victory alone, however. He had the patriarchal mental health system on his side. The system worked beautifully to discount Debbie's nurturing, maternal side as "weakness," and to label her efficiency in managing home, work, and child care as "narcissistic self-involvement." Really! I couldn't believe it, either, when she told me her story and when I read through some of her mental health evaluations (Dan wasn't evaluated!)

Garbage in, garbage out. Isn't that what they say about computers? I say that if clinicians are not trained to understand the feminist issues in women's mental health, women will continue to be victimized. There will be many more Debbies in the years to come.

Can anything be done for the Carols, Joans, and Debbies of this world? Can anything be done to prevent what happened to them from occurring to other innocent women?

I think a great deal can be done. Feminist therapy training should be incorporated into mainstream academic course-work and internship experiences. In therapy, as in any other experience, practitioners see what they look for. If psychiatrists look for "seductive" behavior, they will misinterpret female attractiveness as a "come on," rather than understanding it as a response to a cultural imperative to be "pretty" and "nice." It is also a behavior employed for the purpose of empowerment. Traditionally, the only way a woman had any power was through her attachment to a powerful male protector, whether her father or her husband, and perhaps, her therapist.

Power issues are at the core of women's mental health concerns. If therapists don't understand the effects of felt powerlessness in women, they won't correctly understand women's behavior. They will consistently mislabel, misunderstand, and mistreat female clients. This is an inevitable result of patriarchal training programs.

The study of woman-in-relation must be required for all mental health practitioners. Most women feel a sense of connectedness to other people and to nature. This ability to relate to others, and to the universe, is a unique strength which many men lack because of the individualistic emphasis of our Western culture.

By not understanding the woman-in-relationship, male (and many female) mental health practitioners fail women clients. They misinterpret genuine accounts of abuse as imagined paranoia; they trivialize women's concerns as hysterical emotionalism; they drug and shock women into "adapting" to a culture that disempowers and disaffirms their perceptions and knowledge at every turn.

Self-knowledge is not only lacking, but is a very threatening topic for the dominant, controlling male mental health practitioner. He despises the "weaknesses" of his female clients (while not accepting his own vulnerability.) Individual psychotherapy should be suggested, if not required, for all aspiring therapists while in training. The experience of being a client can be an eye-opener. It teaches one what to do, and more importantly, what not to do—of course a patriarchal, authoritarian training therapist may only teach the student-client to identify with this dominant model.

Cultural influences on women's emotional growth and development are vital to understand. It is no longer enough to know about intra-psychic defense mechanisms, as taught by Freud and his followers. The biological life of women is different from that of men; so is the psychological development of a female child. Women's experience is unique; that uniqueness needs to be affirmed and strengthened. We cannot be molded into man-like creatures, always not measuring up. We can be encouraged and strengthened to develop our own uniqueness, our own gifts.

Those men who work in the "helping professions" must examine their own orientation to their jobs. Do they want to help, or to control? Do they want to share of themselves, or to prop up their sagging egos (and penises) by snickering at their female patients?

Those few therapists who knowingly exploit vulnerable patients again and again must not be allowed to practice in rural America, or anywhere else. The head-in-the-sand posture of most licensing boards is not in the best interests of the profession or the public.

I started out in life accepting without question the "natural order of things"—men as breadwinners, women as homemakers and mothers, supportive of others' goals. It has taken me 60 years to learn that I have a right to be myself—to have my own point of view, and my own valid and experimentally correct truths. These truths will be different from men's truths because they are formed from different physical, emotional, and social experiences than those of men.

"To every thing there is a season, and a time to every purpose under the heaven" (Ecclesiastes 3:1). There was a time I unconditionally
accepted that which I was told was normal or healthy behavior. This
is a different time in my life when I have finally accepted as normal
and healthful my own perceptions, my own experiences, and my
own uniqueness.

The gift that I give my clients is my trust in their own self-knowledge . . . it is the only way to wholeness.

Disclaimer: In order to protect identities of clients, all names and indentify-
ing data have been changed.

V

TRANSITIONS

12

My Symphony

KAYLA MIRIYAM WEINER

My current life as a feminist therapist is like the fourth movement of a symphony. The earlier movements: first my experiences in my Jewish family; second, my work in the civil rights movement as a social activist and my life as an "earth mother"; and third, my doctoral program undertaken in my forties, weave together to create my life now as a professional woman in the world. Now is the time when the themes of the early movements of my life are becoming fully developed and brought to fruition.

The first movement began with darkness. When my mother was 28 years old she contracted a disease (in 1947 usually fatal) that rendered her permanently paralyzed on her left side. She was able to walk only by dragging her left leg, and her left arm was permanently folded across her abdomen. I was five years old at the time, my sister was three and my brother was one. My mother always said she made sure her illness did not impact her children—that we each had a perfectly normal childhood. One does not have to have a doctorate in psychology to realize that having a physically-disabled parent when you are five, with two younger siblings and a father who was essentially absent, would dramatically change one's life. I vividly remember being told on the day my mother came home from the hospital that she had almost died. I realize now how terrifying that was for me. The ways I coped with the fear of abandonment—extreme bravado and mature competency—were to influence me for the rest of my life.

I don't have many memories of growing up because one of my main means of surviving my family experience was to dissociate. I do remember times my mother would cook an elaborate dinner for my father only to have it ruined when he could not get home to eat because business interfered. I watched my disabled mother function as a single parent, getting more and more bitter and unpleasant to my father, and becoming extremely physically and emotionally abusive to me.

At the same time, I was hearing my father and his brothers tell sexist jokes, and I knew they were acquiring "gifts" of women for business clients. When I, as a mature teenager, was used by my uncle as a tool to seduce a business client, I knew something was very wrong. It was many years later that I remembered that my uncle, my father's brother, had sexually abused me as a child.

Because of her condition, my mother was always there when I left or returned to our house. I never knew what kind of mood she would be in—yet I always knew I would bear the brunt of whatever was going on for her. If I was lucky I could make it into my room and stay there until dinner and then return to my room after dinner. If I was not lucky there was a huge fight, usually culminating with me being hit by my mother or father, most frequently with a hair brush or a belt. On some occasions I might get to "zone out" in front of the TV while my father slept in "his" chair and my mother read or knitted. I do not remember us ever listening to music together, playing games, or having any conversation that was not a fight or argument.

I began to work with my father in his business when I was in high school and two things became quite clear to me. One was that I was very good in the business world. The other was that there was no way I could be involved in that world because it was reserved for the men in the family. All my life it had been assumed I would go to college; the only question seemed to be whether I would become a nurse or a teacher. There was never another option. I eventually chose teaching because I had been convinced as I was growing up that I was "great with kids." I decided to teach elementary school because I had also been convinced I was not smart enough to teach any other subject.

After two years in the elementary education curriculum, at a time when I thought I would be bored out of my mind, I transferred into a secondary education program with a major in English and a minor in

Social Studies. I began to thrive in that program. When I graduated I contracted to teach in a junior high school in Philadelphia's inner city and then went to Europe for the summer. To my shock and amazement, while I was away on my graduation trip my parents called the school district and informed them I would not be teaching. My parents did not want me associating with people of color because they feared I might become romantically involved with someone of color!

Before I go to the next movement of the symphony it is important for me to describe the background theme threading it's way through the first movement. One must be able to "hear" the experience of my life in the Jewish community.

My Judaism was a big part of my growing up—in a religious, cultural and ethnic sense. I attended or taught Sunday School most of my life. I learned that one of the most important concepts of Judaism is *Tikkun Olum*. Roughly translated this means *"to repair and make whole the world."* I was taught that to be a good Jew it is more important to do *Mitzvah* (good deeds) and practice *Tikkun olum*, than to do any other of the teachings of Judaism. I believe that. My parents taught that all people are good and one should look for the best in all people. I believe that too. It was with the job cancellation that I finally came to realize that what my parents really meant—even if they didn't realize it—was that all people are good—if they were rich, white, and Jewish. I couldn't live with the contradictions.

The week I returned from Europe, the week classes were to begin in all the school districts in the area, I secured a teaching position in a suburban school district that had a very white student and teacher population. Within two months of starting my new job I moved out of my parent's home, bought my first car and rented my first apartment.

I learned a lot about education and about the world during my first professional appointment. Some of the people I met almost 30 years ago are still in my life. In the "lily white" school district where I was teaching, the three black teachers all became my friends and my teachers. One was active in the Black Power movement and guided me to my involvement in the civil rights movement. For many years I worked in white communities, educating about racism and organizing groups to support the activities of people of color.

My experience in the civil rights movement precipitated my path down the road to feminism. Working in the civil rights movement was a real eye-opener, as so many of us found out at the time. Yes, we women could make the signs and type the flyers and hand out literature, but when it came to decisions—well, the guys thought they could do it better. I vividly remember sitting at my first "CR" group. Two feminists had come to speak. They were anything but "feminine" as I then understood the word and I leaned over to a friend and asked her the meaning of "feminism". She explained it meant working for equal rights for women—and my head exploded with "clicks!!!" All of the cognitive dissonance cleared up. I understood!! I had been told I was as good as everyone but as I learned then—"everyone is created equal" had been meant for rich, white Christian males. It was clearly an illusion to think that I, as a middle class Jewish female was meant to be included.

My family and my selected community had been shown to be hypocritical. I decided to run away. I purchased a van, took my dog and two cats and started out across the country with no job and no destination. I worked as a waitperson in various resorts getting a real taste of the oppression and paternalism that runs rampant in that occupation. While hiking in the Grand Canyon I met a man whom I married two months later on the rim of the Grand Canyon. Together we moved to Montana where we bought 85 acres of land and built a large, six sided log home. I learned to do concrete work, electricity, plumbing, mechanics and all the things necessary to build and operate a farm. This "little girl" from the city who thought radishes grew in bunches, eventually learned, among other things, to milk cows, birth lambs, shear sheep, raise bees for honey and grow and preserve most of her own food including making ketchup from homegrown tomatoes and butter from raw milk!

While I lived in the country I continued to work with women's issues, peace issues and environmental issues. I worked as a counselor in a home for delinquent youth and I was a resource person in my self-created women's center in NW Montana. Amidst the new learning and hard work of rural life I had time to reflect upon the sexism and anti-Semitism I had experienced in the world and integrate that into an analysis of sexism and racism in the world. I also had the opportunity to observe economic oppression from the underside. I had the opportunity to pull my experiences together and further develop my analysis of the interrelationship of all oppression.

After ten years of living on my mountain retreat, I left and returned to the city. My plan was to reinforce my counseling skills (I had gotten a M.Ed. while I was teaching) with the intent of going back to Montana and Idaho to serve as counselor to the abused women I saw around me. I entered a master's degree program but was told I did not belong there because I had too much knowledge and too much experience. It took me about six months to really hear and accept the fact that I was being advised to enter a doctoral program. My own internalized sexism had me saying, "Who me?" Well, yes me. Shortly thereafter I entered an external doctoral degree program, opened a private practice in feminist therapy, and divorced the man I had married.

My work in those years was truly transformative. The women I met through *The Union Institute* (my graduate school) and at the annual conferences of the Association for Women in Psychology (AWP) provided a container to nurture me through what was to be a life transformation. These women, Penny Mac-Elveen Hoehn, Lee Piper, Miriam Kieffer, Ellyn Kaschak and Mavis Tsai—along with my personal friends—were a part of the minuet of my life symphony—there to move me to where I am personally and professionally today.

I clearly remember going to my first AWP meeting. Someone had suggested it as a good place to find feminist therapists to serve on my doctoral committee. As I went from one session to another I was quite dismayed because it seemed everyone was talking about object relations theory. I knew that wasn't theoretically or practically what I believed was good for women. Then I found Ellyn. I agreed with everything I heard her say; she became one of my mentors, and through her I found the community with which I could identify, learn and grow. For the next several years, while I was doing my graduate work, AWP became my professional socializing tool. It was in that safe environment that I learned how to submit a proposal and give a paper at a conference. It was there I made contacts with other women of like mind. It was within AWP that I developed the Jewish Women's Caucus and had the opportunity to contribute an article entitled *Anti-Semitism in The Therapy Room* to the book (inspired by the Caucus), *Jewish Women In Therapy: Seen But Not Heard*, 1991, edited by Rachel Josefowitz Siegel and Ellen Cole, Binghamton: Haworth. It was also through my work with the caucus that I conceived the idea of the *First International Conference on Judaism, Feminism and Psychology: Creating a Shelter in the Wilderness*. Many others helped me give birth to the conference in October, 1992 in Seattle, Washington, which has in turn given birth to much action around the country and around the world, addressing the issues of the psychology of Jewish women. In addition, I have co-edited a book of papers from the conference entitled *Jewish Women Speak Out: Expanding the Boundaries of Psychology.*

The final movement of my symphony began when I was diagnosed with breast cancer in December, 1989. There is no way to describe what it means to hear that diagnosis except to say that it is something akin to being in the water and hearing someone shout "SHARK!" I was very lucky. My diagnosis came very early by way of an extremely diligent radiologist who read my annual mammogram carefully, and because of a competent pathologist and brilliant surgeon. Even though my prognosis is excellent—99% chance of no recurrence, I am fully aware that I *live with cancer on a daily basis.*

My life in my family of origin, my life as a liberal political activist and radical feminist, my life as a married farmer, and my life as a single woman with cancer, all inform my work as a feminist therapist. The years have helped me to understand my mother's losses and pain and my father's burdens and combine to temper my own hurts with compassion and understanding. I am able to use my own healing to help clients learn to reject the pain of their abuse, and embrace, when appropriate, the love that may be found within their family. My years on the farm gave me a rural life experience along with a multitude of images that I now use as metaphors in my therapy work. My political activity, liberal and radical, has made me sensitive to the slightest indication of externalized or internalized oppression and allows me to aid the growth and development of my clients to include an understanding of the significance of oppression in the world and in their lives.

Living with cancer has profoundly changed my life. I still believe that *tikkun olum* is the most important thing I can do in life and I still continue to work to transform the world. I do my work with an understanding and passion about making my life whole. I go through life now, doing my work at home and at the office and in the world always realizing how very blessed I have been and I look forward to each day with joy and enthusiasm to the coda of my life.

13

The Natural History of a Feminist Therapy

ADRIENNE J. SMITH

I think I was always a feminist, just as I think I was always a lesbian—though I didn't know either fact about my identity until my mid-20s for the latter and the mid-30s for the former. When I was in high school I wrote an essay on women doctors—the first clear evidence of my feminism. And I somehow always knew that I would never marry but I would be a doctor, (as it turned out, a Ph.D. rather than an M.D.).

After finishing my degree in 1966, well before the second wave of feminism began, I took various workshops in different therapeutic approaches, becoming particularly interested in Adler's ideas, which I have since adopted into my version of feminist therapy. Although I couldn't articulate it, I was dissatisfied with what I had learned. In 1972, while I was still working at the VA, I became intrigued with the feminist readings my lover was bringing home from the sociology classes she was taking. As for many women, feminism "exploded" in me, making sense, finally, of my feelings of being a misfit. After seven or eight attempts at psychotherapy (I had lost count), feminism "cured" me. I was so taken that I thought of little else.

That year I was program chair of the Illinois Group Psychotherapy Society and, with my new found awareness, realized that there had never been an all-women panel discussing feminist ideas. In my nai-vite I called Naomi Wiesstein who was then on the faculty of Loyola University of Chicago and convinced her to appear on the panel. She insisted on the appearance of several other women she named, none I had ever heard of, including Pauline Bart, Marlyn Grossman and Anne Sieden. Each of them agreed although at the last minute Naomi was unable to attend. That all-day panel started my involvement in the Chicago feminist movement.

Almost instantly I was on panels, speaking at meetings and forums and expounding on feminist therapy (although I had not heard that phrase). It seemed that I "knew" on some deep level of my being what it meant to be a woman, whether married or not, lesbian or not. For example, when I was asked to speak louder at one large meeting. I responded with: "That's what happens because we've been trained not to speak up" and just about brought the house down. No one had taught me this, I found it in my very soul, stimulated by the reading I was doing voraciously and the women I was meeting.

During that year I also began to make tentative moves toward coming out as a lesbian (I had lived a VERY closeted life since meeting my lover in 1959). Finally I decided to risk it—I quit my job and started a full time practice as an open lesbian feminist therapist. Since I was, and remained for many years, the only openly lesbian Ph.D.-level therapist in Chicago, I not only quickly built up a thriving practice but became the "expert" on many panels, workshops, and radio and TV shows. I became involved with Chicago Women Against Rape and often spoke on their behalf.

In 1973 my newly-formed alliances with the Chicago feminist therapy community led to my attending one of the first meetings of the Association for Women In Psychology (AWP), held in the auditorium of a University of Illinois Medical School building. I have attended almost every AWP meeting since then and have been thrilled by its growth.

Also in 1973 I was talked into attending the APA meeting in Montreal. I had attended a few APA's as a graduate student and young professional but found them so alienating that I had not attended for several years. Well! That Montreal APA was one of the most exciting events of my life! I was high the entire week.

It was at that meeting that Division 35 was formally accepted as a division and that the Association of Gay Psychologists (now the Association of Lesbian and Gay Psychologists—ALGP—was formed). I was at the very first meeting of ALGP and I cannot begin to convey the thrill, the joy, the feeling of finally having my most important identities, as a psychologist and a lesbian, recognized simultaneously. I spent my time at that convention between the AWP suite and the ALGP group. I'll never forget those years of being part of a group of open lesbians and gay men presenting to the Open Forum a carefully planned list of demands on behalf of ALGP. Since that date I've only missed two APA meetings, both from necessity. Also, since that date I've been involved in one form or another with ALGP, was on first Executive Committee when Division 44 (Division of Lesbian and Gay Issues) was formally approved and served as President of Div 44 from 1988–1990.

Since 1973 both halves of my professional identity have grown in parallel. It was also at the 1973 APA convention that I first met Hannah Lerman and Ella Lasky, among many other feminist therapists. We began to talk about our budding practices and new philosophy of therapy and decided, then and there, to present a panel at the Midwinter meeting of Division 29 (Psychotherapy) in San Diego, March 1974. We divided the topic into arbitrary thirds, each taking one piece, and met again in San Diego. Hannah lives in Los Angeles, Ella in New York, and I in Chicago. We had not consulted since our meeting in Montreal but in San Diego we presented papers that were almost interchangeable. What a testimony to the grass roots growth of feminist therapy ideas! And what public misunderstanding we evoked! A reporter from the local newspaper, a woman who was, in fact, quite interested and sympathetic to our views, quoted one of us as defining a feminist therapist as "a woman who loves women". (Although some of us do, that is not enough to make any of us feminist therapists!) Of course, at that early date, none of us, nor anyone else, had received any training in feminist therapy. We created it out of our experience as therapists and our growing consciousness of feminism.

I developed my philosophy and practice of feminist therapy from a combination of Rogerian, Adlerian, and radical therapy. My role-models, through reading only, included Frieda Fromm-Reichman and Hogie Wyckoff. Gradually over the years I have developed a theory of feminist therapy which is based in my belief in the individual's (both male and female) need to survive under whatever conditions s/he finds him or her self and to achieve some power over one's own life.. I see ALL behavior as developed for that purpose (here I incorporate Adlerian purposefulness). As a feminist I believe that each sex is conditioned by the gendered experiences of childhood and the present. Because women and girls have not been allowed overt power we have developed many covert styles of achieving some type of personal, life-preserving power. These forms have traditionally been called "manipulative," "underhanded," "sneaky," "feminine wiles" and other pejorative phrases. My job, as a feminist therapist, is to introduce this idea to women (and to men the obverse, that their power is also restricted by the demand to be macho) thus empowering them and reducing guilt. I also "teach", through example, within the therapeutic relationship, and by direct re-framing of their experiences, other ways of using power and offer them the choice. Early in my practice I referred several women clients to a therapy group run by a colleague who reported that one woman had characterized the difference between feminist therapy and traditional therapies she had experienced as "Adrienne focuses on my strengths, other therapists always focused on my weaknesses." My theory of therapy is more completely developed in *Feminist Therapy: Redefining power for the powerless* and in *Empowerment as an ethical imperative.*

Because very early in my practice I did not understand the limits essential to good therapy, I tended to go overboard with sharing power and self-disclosure. My clients knew more about me than was necessary and I now realize that I often interrupted their process with my own "stuff." I also socialized with clients, not understanding the need to maintain some distinction between roles. I have also tried to barter goods and services for therapy but found that, with the exception of a few unusual clients, the two roles do not mix. It's almost impossible to act as someone's boss and, later that week, become the non-judgmental mental therapist. Two incidents of mixing roles turned out splendidly and I am very proud of them. In one my colleague, Ruth Siegel, and I had led a therapy group for lesbian couples. During the year long existence of the group one of the members, who had leukemia, became ever sicker and, at the end of the group, died. The group members became her support group but, more importantly, supported the well partner and in so doing learned about guilty self-sacrifice versus needful self-care. When she died, we met, at the request of the group, for a final session where all of us, members and therapists, simply sat silently in a circle on the floor listening to Bach. We then all attended the funeral and created our own feminist space by moving the chairs from their rigidly placed rows into a circle. One of the family members commented that she had never attended a lesbian funeral before and she liked it! The part of which I am most proud, however, came a year later. Ruth and I invited the surviving lover, who was also a therapist, to present a workshop with us about the group and her experiences. This we did in 1982 at the Div. 29 Midwinter meeting in Mexico City. The workshop was hugely successful and the survivor made another step in her working-through of her loss.

Several years later I again invited clients to present with me. This time it was a couple whose marriage had been greatly improved through our work together. We three wrote the paper jointly, each of us speaking in our own voice from our particular perspective. We then presented our experiences at an international conference and again were received very positively. In fact, the couple was deluged with questions and interest. Several women said they wished their husbands would work with them in therapy with as much willingness as this man had.

As I have matured I still self-disclose, but am much more aware of when it is appropriate and when I'm intruding on the client's process. Several years ago my mother died and I flew to the funeral, necessitating several days off work. Of course, I shared this with my clients and I recall one in particular who had just lost her own mother. We cried together and mutually comforted each other.

I have had several clients "come on to me" sexually, including one who asked if I had ever been sexually attracted to a client. I answered truthfully that I had but that my ethics (and I did not add, my common sense) dictated firm boundaries. Years later she thanked me for not giving in to her rather intense and prolonged attempt to seduce me.

Perhaps the most unexpected response to a self-disclosure came from a male client who finally got up the courage to ask if I were lesbian. When I confirmed it he grinned and visibly relaxed, saying, "Thank heaven. Now I won't have to play any sexual games with you." What an opening for me to challenge his need to deal with all women only through their aspect as sexual objects.

My countertransference issues occur around sexual attraction, over-identification, especially with lesbians, psychologists and activists, and blurring of roles. I have been very lucky to work with a wonderful, straight colleague, Ruth F. Siegel, with whom I have co-presented numerous workshops and panels and co-wrote a chapter outlining our theory of power in feminist therapy. (See reference list at end of this article.) Her presence in my working day enables me to consult with her whenever I encounter a sticky countertransference issue. She has saved me from many foolish mistakes.

Since I have been fairly active in the local lesbian and feminist communities I have had some rather interesting and amusing client responses. Several clients have expressed jealousy of my lover. There is, of course, the question of meeting clients in other settings, For example, once, after a concert, a client came for her appointment angry and moving the chairs from their rigidly placed rows into a circle. She claimed I had hugged others but not her, that I had paid more attention to others. I had no memory of this and gradually we worked it out.

One other time a client who was at the same meeting as I commented on how smooth and comfortable my comments seemed to be compared to her tension and anxiety when she wished to make a comment. This led to a very fruitful discussion on the inner feelings versus the outer appearance. Happily, I have been able to turn all such incidents into fuel for therapeutic work. I have been involved in several feminist and feminist therapy organizations but the one with which I most identify is the Feminist Therapy Institute (FTI) of which I am a co-founder. FTI grew out of a need that several of us "older" feminist therapists felt when we went to AWP or APA or other professional meetings and found ourselves repeatedly explaining "feminist therapy 101" to eager young women. There was no organization where we could share experiences with older, experienced feminist therapists so we created one. FTI is now 10 years old (as of 1992). We have had 10 very successful conferences and published two books to which I have contributed three chapters (see references). We have developed a feminist code of ethics that stresses pro-action rather than prohibitions.

I believe feminist therapy, as I define it, is vital to people who have been for too long labeled as pathological when all they are is gendered people struggling to maintain some modicum of personal power under oppressive conditions. The most negative impression I have heard about feminist therapy, an extension of people's misconceptions about feminism in general, is that we are simply preaching another type of orthodoxy. I have had occasional clients, usually straight women, ask my permission for them to wear lipstick or skirts. We are currently seeing a rush to deny what is seen as the pressure for women to work outside the home. As with all attempts to counter one apparently oppressive situation, there is now the opposite oppression happening, and women are pressured to have children, and to do it all. Feminist therapy could go far toward releasing women from the pressure to conform to any set of "shoulds" but it must be especially careful not to impose a new set.

Recently I have been involved in a project of which I am very proud. I am one of three co-editors of an anthology entitled *Lesbians At Midlife: The Creative Transition* (see references). Since publication in January, 1991, this book has received excellent reviews and made two bookstore bestseller lists. I have also been exploring my Jewish roots and have written a chapter on that in *Jewish Women in Therapy: Seen But Not Heard* (see references).

In July 1990, I was diagnosed with colon cancer. After surgery it was clear that the cancer had metastasized to my liver. So, in November I ended my practice and am living a retired life. As of this writing (1992) I am still healthy and active, thanks to a combination of a macrobiotic diet, Chinese herbs, vitamins and supplements and chemotherapy. I have bought a motor-home and am busily driving around the country and enjoying it immensely. The cancer has led me to a total change in my way of life and to a gradual re-evaluation of my life's goals and purposes. I don't know who or what I'll be next year or thereafter but the search and new awareness is very exciting—and humbling. It was rather a shock, for example, to learn, not just academically but through my own gut, how much emotional 'feeding' one gets from clients. The self-imposed lack of that source of supply has forced me to turn more to friends and family and, especially, to myself. So I am a soul in process. Where the process will carry me is the next, as yet unwritten, chapter.

REFERENCES

Smith, A. J. & Siegel, R. F. (1985) *Feminist therapy: Redefining power for the powerless.* In L. B. Rosewater & L. E. A. Walker (eds.) *HANDBOOK OF FEMINIST THERAPY.* New York, Springer.

Smith, A. J.(1990) *Working within the lesbian community: The dilemma of overlapping relationships.* In H.Lerman & N.Porter (Eds.) *FEMINIST ETHICS IN PSYCHOTHERAPY.* New York, Springer.

Smith, A. J. & Douglas, M. A. (1990) *Empowerment as an ethical imperative.* In H. Lerman & N. Porter (Eds.) *FEMINIST ETHICS IN PSYCHOTHERAPY.* New York, Springer.

Sang, B., Warshow, J. and Smith,A. J. (Eds.) (1991) *LESBIANS AT MIDLIFE: THE CREATIVE TRANSITION.* San Francisco, Spinsters Book Company.

Smith, A. J. (1991) *Reflections of a Jewish Lesbian-Feminist Activist-Therapist; or, First of All I Am Jewish, the Rest is Commentary.* In R. J. Siegel and E. Cole (Eds.) *JEWISH WOMEN IN THERAPY: SEEN BUT NOT HEARD.* New York, Haworth Press.

14

The Paradox of One-to-One Therapy: A Personal Feminist History

POLLY TAYLOR

I worked as a psychotherapist in child guidance and private practice from the late 1950s until 1977, when I closed my practice and went looking for the Older Women's Movement (by which I meant women over forty) and the Feminist Therapy Movement. Since I haven't practiced since, I am now a "relict" of a time when feminist therapy was a dream in the minds of isolated therapists here and there around the world.

It was the contradictions between feminism and therapy which led me to leave the latter and concentrate on the former. Perhaps these contradictions have all been resolved and my reminiscences are only of historical interest. If so, take my words as a glimpse of what was and an opportunity to renew our commitment to what feminist therapy has come to be.

I grew up in a many-generations-of-Quakers community near Philadelphia, where I was born in 1929, and spent my high school years in a Quaker boarding school. I learned, as an ideal, respect for people and for our ability to direct our own lives. From a young age, I knew and admired people whose lives were devoted to fighting against oppression. Whether or not I succeeded at it, I knew what kind of person I wanted to be—one I could be proud of. My siblings were all married with children about the time I started college and I had no interest in being a homemaker. I wanted to be out in the world; using my mind. I never wanted to have children of my own because of my severe, and hereditary, allergies.

In the 1950s, after working in child care for a few years, I was trained as a social worker in a Freudian school. The psychiatric specialization concentrated on neuroses. We believed in a sort of universal solvent—the one on one, woman to woman relationship dissolving the tangles left from infancy and allowing the client to live the fullest life of which he (sic) was capable. I also learned the original magic of Freudian psychology—to listen.

The 1950s were a terrible time for the mental health of women. Tremendous demands were made on mothers to do a perfect job of raising children, with little or no community support. In addition, the nuclear family pattern isolated women from their mothers and other role models. Psychology was very popular as an explanation of women's despair but it had little to offer beyond diagnostic labels. Very rich women could go into analysis; very desperate women, with symptoms which disrupted the family, were hospitalized. Child guidance clinics such as the ones where I worked were an answer for some because women could take their children there without challenging society's construct of the family. Once there, "the mother" had access to treatment for herself. Essentially, those of us who worked woman-to-woman in the clinics were bootlegging help to the women.(Eventually, we were found out. I left my last agency job because funds were available only for seeing children!)

I felt very good about my work. My clients grew to understand how their circumstances affected their lives and that gave a tremendous boost to their self-esteem, confidence, and ability to cope. Many of them made tremendous progress in overcoming the anxiety, depression, and so-called neurotic symptoms that were natural results of living in an emotional desert. Until the Women's Liberation Movement expanded our ambitions and our expectations, that was a lot!

During that time, outside my office, I was involved in mind-bending social changes—union struggles, the civil rights movement, the anti-war movement, the use of mind-altering drugs, the upsurge of interest in Eastern philosophies and practices, and the new human potential schools of therapy. Women emerged as impressive, inspiring figures in all those movements. But, in spite of my commitment and my activism, these societal changes were somewhere outside of my own life; each was for me what we called, in my school days, an extra-curricular activity. I used some of my skills, as in working with conscientious objectors and writing reports about draftees' families, but my involvements did not change my life OR my professional skills and body of knowledge.

I became active in the Women's Liberation Movement initially around the legalization of abortion. As a feminist, I maintained my active commitment to social change. What was new was that my political awareness led to changes in my own life and work. I loved being a feminist because it tied my personal, professional, and political lives together.

Years of doing marital and parent counseling and working with teenage "girls" had made the oppression of women in the family vivid to me. But it was feminism which first focused on what I myself had in common with those women—what women had in common regardless of education, regardless of jobs or careers, regardless of sexual preference or family relationships. Before the consciousness-raising groups, I was some kind of hybrid of the working man and the mothering woman. Feminism gave the label "sexism" to my colleagues who disregarded or discounted me and for the general run of folk who saw me as "unfulfilled." Suddenly, my choices for myself were legitimized; I was a strong woman rather than a social deviant. I was one of millions of women oppressed in a variety of ways. I was no longer doing it wrong while "the mothers" did it right.

Since I was a therapist and now a feminist, I would be a feminist therapist! I called myself that, and selected and worked with clients on that basis for several years, roughly from 1970 to 1977. But the feminists I admired most declared that women's problems came from oppression and that our energy needed to be directed to combating oppressive societal attitudes, institutions, and behavior.

In the first flush of feminist enthusiasm it seemed to me that the new understanding of ourselves as women should expand and enrich my professional practice. I knew from psychiatric lore that the client's development of strength and independent health is vital. To feminism, this same goal was an absolute essential. Weren't both theories pointing the same way? If my therapy helped, wouldn't my clients develop self-definitions as women, according to their own ethnicity, as autonomous individuals? Wasn't there a need for some feminists to put our energy into individual work?

My radical feminist cohorts said no. They did not trust trained, experienced therapy as a tool in the Women's Liberation Movement. Psychiatry denied the importance of external, political influences and did not challenge the sexist and abusive attitudes of men. Women were blamed for problems that arose from the pressure of society's demands. We were urged to seek insight and to change ourselves as the (individual) solution to our "complaints." If women were angry about this blaming, we were told our neurotic patterns were making us hostile and that we needed to change ourselves still more. The Women's Movement debunked this, saying that changes needed to be made in the oppressive society we lived in.

In my day-to-day practice I was most aware of the disparity in these theories as they applied to relationships between women. On the one horn of the dilemma was the egalitarian commitment of Women's Studies and the Consciousness-Raising groups. On the other horn were my training and experience—to be objective, to exert minimal influence on the client, to allow myself to be an object of transference. The egalitarian style felt right; therapeutic lack of involvement, the vicissitudes of transference, and the contradiction of interminable therapy had always troubled me. I disliked the pedestal. The knowledge that women had of themselves was far more impressive to me than what the psychiatric texts said. Putting the clients' awareness into my practice seemed the surest way of doing good work. But my therapeutic experience had taught me the value of emotional detachment—of being the secure, strong, somewhat anonymous anchor for the client to cling to in the face of seemingly uncontrollable, and unacceptable, emotional storms.

Nothing I tried resolved the contradiction I saw between respect for women and the competent therapeutic role—the "paradox" of my story's title. No matter how much I, and many of my clients, struggled to achieve equality in the treatment setting, the mystique of the therapist hung between us. My clients had been well-trained to look to the expert for guidance and understanding and I had been trained to exercise all my knowledge and experience. But there was more to it than that. I would have to find new ways of working if I were to abandon the mask of knowing and meet my clients as equals in the therapy. Equality without a new discipline could mean sharing my problems and personal insecurities and adding to the burdens of the clients. Sharing could also mean it would be obvious what I thought, for example, of the way some guy treated my client. If economic factors, or family commitments, or her fear of being on her own, or the myth of being no one without a man made leaving impossible, my scorn for him could prevent my supporting her to find her own way.

I undertook a number of projects in the attempt to overcome the contradictions between my feminist and professional insights. I became active in a group devoted to defining and identifying feminist practice in the therapeutic community. Half of us were practicing therapists; half of us were psychiatric "patients" determined to tackle the abuses which had characterized their therapy. In matched pairs, we interviewed any therapist (starting with our own therapist-members) who wanted to be listed as a feminist therapist. Many practitioners wanted to be interviewed and wanted to talk about how to help women. Most of them were very hesitant about discussing therapeutic technique with defined "patients." Almost all of them were patronizing. The matched pairs trick was a great revealer; almost all the interviewees addressed almost all their remarks to the "therapist" interviewer. (Perhaps having our roles anonymous would have been interesting, but in a small city the therapists all knew at least the names of the other therapists and it was more important to us to have immediate evidence of a therapist's response to a "patient.") We ended up adding a few more women to our group but developing only a very small, largely inexperienced pool of feminist therapists. The experience drew me further into feminism and made me more critical of basic mental health thinking.

Continuing my search for solutions, I found another contradiction. As a feminist I was working to encourage, mirror, exemplify the autonomy of women—our right to participate in decisions affecting us, to give weight to our own preferences, and to express our own ethnicity and individuality. But the client leaving my office often found no community. In fact, the community was poised ready to punish the woman who came out as a "women's libber." The social structures my clients needed weren't developed yet.

The women's movement was developing consciousness-raising and support groups, which were a great help to all of us who saw ourselves as feminists. Unfortunately, they reflected the women who were at the forefront. The groups were, or at least appeared, academic in their theoretical expression, oriented to students and others with university affiliation, based on an understanding of left-wing political ideologies, and unable to relate to family and financial ob-

ligations. Many of my clients were older and did not have that kind
of academic understanding; they had children and parents to support. My feminist emphasis on their personhood energized them to
go out and hit their heads on brick walls.

I was faced with this contradiction between feminism and therapy
in my own office as well as in both feminist gatherings and professional affiliations. I chose the new understanding and began moving
away from one-on-one, woman to woman, internally-focused, traditional therapy practice. I went looking for ways to include the political in my work—to address the causal impact of community and
society, and develop a broader awareness of the client's set and setting. I was involved in numerous humanistic, personal-growth
training opportunities where I learned new techniques for involving
clients in their own treatment. Many of the new schools challenged
traditional treatment modalities in effective and appropriate ways.
None of them challenged society's traditional male-centered base.

Since consciousness-raising groups had helped me struggle with
oppressive sexism in my personal life, I hoped a similar approach
could help in my professional struggle. I set about gathering feminists who were therapists to talk together. Only a couple of the
women who responded had anywhere near the amount of professional experience I had. Most were very strong feminists but beginning therapists. Working with them was great fun because they had
the feminist principles so firmly in their minds and could identify
very quickly the dangerous elitism in therapeutic methods. But they
did not see the dangers of deserting the detachment and strength of
the therapist's role. While I benefited from their attention to women
and they probably benefited from my knowledge of therapy, I didn't
find the reinforcement of other experienced therapists that I needed
so badly. Nor did I find a way to develop appropriate therapeutic
techniques.

I also joined a teaching group, sponsored by the Women's Studies
College, to put on a seminar in feminist therapy. We wrestled with
the interface between feminism and therapy—in our meetings and
in the classroom. But we discovered only questions. It was too soon,
if not inherently impossible, to establish an integration.

By this time, I was happier than ever with my own life—with coming out as a lesbian, with struggling in a wider political arena, with
really looking at my professional practice. And I was increasingly
discouraged and disillusioned with the profession. The last bit of
awareness to get through to me was that, as a feminist, I needed to

consider my own feelings and my own physical needs, to drop the "at your service" mentality and pay attention to my own life. My age, my disability, and my lesbian preference all needed to be part of my work and my politics. My allergies had always been with me. I had been passing (dreaming up excuses to get out of places where I'd get sick) since I was in Kindergarten. Now menopause and the increase in environmental chemicals were making it harder to pass. It had finally gotten through to me that I could design MY life, that I need not play the role of (isn't it a shame) unmarried professional woman with weird limitations, which I had drifted into years before.

So I sold almost everything I owned and left home. I ran away with my lover in a twenty-three-foot motor home, storing only 43 cartons of books (three cartons were mine), and headed for the promised land, looking for the Older Women's Movement.

Of course, there were other factors in my leaving my private practice and migrating to California. The weather in '77 was worse than ever, the political weather wasn't any better, my lover couldn't find a job that reflected her interests and convictions, and I wanted to chuck it all, including middle class possessions and affiliations.

My initial intent was to find other therapists for whom feminism was important and to continue my career in a more congenial community. I spent time, here and there across the country, with women who seemed to share my interest, but did NOT find women who had resolved my dilemmas. I found, as I had in Buffalo, women struggling to be both feminist and therapist and being pushed out of the movement because they were therapists and out of the therapeutic community because they were feminists. Also, my new life, as an itinerant with a dramatically decreased income and no established relationships, gave me a glimpse of further contradictions to come— especially around class and race.

Absorbed in political protest and new adventures, I scarcely noticed that a year had gone by and my license had lapsed. Nor did it occur to me to try to renew or transfer it. I never looked for professional work. My attention was on feminism and I was delighted to look for a more menial way to support myself. I haven't regretted the change. My health is better than it would have been had I stayed in the East. My financial state is poor, but maybe it would have been anyway. My emotional, social, political life is infinitely better. I found mid-life and long-living women struggling to be heard and women who were ready to support me (as they have ever since) in working to get us heard as feminists over forty. Through and with them, I found work to do, in editing and publishing BROOMSTICK, which satisfied my need for making a meaningful contribution. I control my own environment pretty well. I left the mental health field because of the contradictions. I had not found a way to help clients be more liberated and still survive in the community. I had not found support from other therapists for myself. I had not found a way to avoid the mystique of being the therapist vis-a-vis the (less knowledgeable) client. I had not found a way to take care of my own environmental illness and still conduct a practice.

I certainly hope the options for feminists who are or want to be therapists are better now. I'm also sure that there are millions of people out there, even in the therapeutic community, who haven't changed their minds in twenty years. I suspect the contradictions between the egalitarian principles of feminism and the expertise of professional psychology still exact a price. There is a lot of work to be done in addressing society as a whole and any progress made in blending psychological understanding, therapeutic skills, and feminist theory can only help.

Epilogue

In the years since the therapists in this book began their practices, women's psychological situations have not vastly changed. A client of mine relates that her husband treats her like a child (she is a businesswoman of 32) by requiring that she pledge to him that she will not buy any more new clothes although they do not discuss what *he* will do to reduce expenses. (Their combined salaries bring in well over $100,000 a year.) When she gets angry at this and other put-downs and petty rules, he claims she is "being emotional," thus "proving" her incompetence to make reasonable demands and decisions. Women who bring charges of sexual harassment or rape are still being called "crazy," "provocative" and "rejected lovers." Clinicians still willfully ignore the data from thousands of studies of women's histories and treat their female clients as if their claims of sexual assault by father, brother, uncles, and therapists are somehow their fault or false. Many states still have not criminalized sexual acting out by a therapist against his client. (Although sexual activity between female therapists and their clients occurs, it is rare.)

Equally retrograde are the numbers of books and articles pitched to women that encourage them to minimize, if not ignore, the effects of socialization on personality. Women (and very young girls) are still being urged to lose weight, to do away with wrinkles, to suction off body fat, and augment breasts. Nowhere is it mentioned in these messages that the desired results have been defined by men, to please men. An article in the sports section of *The New York Times* (Feb. 9,1992) describes the despair of some high-powered professional basketball players that their "dancing girls" (cheerleaders) were not dressed in "revealing enough" costumes. While the money assigned to *women's* professional sports is pitifully low.

Disheartening to me are the numbers of books that are meant to be helpful to women but are almost all "recovery" books. Women need to recover all right, not from their "addictions" but from their socialization. Yet the books on feminist psychology take up one-half a shelf in our local "feminist" bookstore, while the books on "recovery" take up several book-*cases!* That was my moment of truth, leading to this book.

Where are the books that will let women know that a psychotherapy was invented for them more than 20 years ago, and still exists, that does not sexually exloit them, that does not relegate them to dependent "advice-seeker" status, and does not compound their view of themselves as "sick" and addicted to neurotic behaviors or to causing others to behave in destructive and self-destructive ways? Feminist therapy is completely unique in helping women trust in their own basic mental health while at the same time offering counseling for emotional distress. Feminist therapy does not, like therapies based on "goddess" theories, imply that women must contact their archetypal blueprints in order to be mentally healthy. On the contrary, feminist therapy suggests that such "archetypes" are completely defined by patriarchal societies to teach women how limited their spheres of influence must be—and how separate from men's! Feminist therapy does not encourage women to shed neurotic patterns of self-defeating behavior to "get in touch with the good feelings within." Feminist therapists know that there are few good feelings to get in touch with inside a girl who has been raped by a family-member, who has grown up deprived of self-esteem from her culture or left pregnant, or worse, by a boy who loved her "too much to let a condom get in the way of our closeness," as one boy told a newspaper reporter when he was asked if Magic Johnson's anouncement that he was HIV-positive persuaded him to use condoms. "Getting in touch with the good feelings within" is a destructive suggestion that is basically religious in nature. It has little to do with the original causes of girls' and women's bad feelings.

Only feminist therapy remains committed to bringing about the insight in women that the solutions to the many emotional burdens they carry lay in social and political change—in women co-operating with each other to urge lawmakers to pay attention to their everyday needs: for low-cost, safe day-care, for access to positions of power and the money to fund their political campaigns, for safe abortions and user-friendly birth control for teens that does not require a gynecology degree or the male's participation.

Only feminist therapy reminds women that they are not responsible for the mental illness, addictions, or criminality in their children and love partners. Only feminist therapy urges women to look at their families, their histories and at their society, not in the mirror, to discover the sources of their low self-esteem—if, indeed, it is low.

Only feminist therapy, of all therapies, directs women in emotional distress away from magical thinking about archetypes, past-lives, inner conflicts, biological determinism and its concomitant, sexual separatism, to contemplate the effects on them of the low value still assigned to them by their culture. The work of feminist therapy is still valid, still needed, and largely, still unknown.